D1196148

© Copyright 2000
by
Krause Publications

All rights reserved.

No portion of this publication may be reproduced or transmitted in any form or by any means, electronic or mechanical, including photocopy, recording, or any information storage and retrieval system, without permission in writing from the publisher, except by a reviewer who may quote brief passages in a critical article or review to be printed in a magazine or newspaper, or electronically transmitted on radio or television.

krause
publications

700 East State Street • Iola, WI 54990-0001
715/445-2214 • FAX: 715/445-4087   www.krause.com

Published by
700 E. State St.
Iola, WI 54990-0001
Telephone 715-445-2214
www.krause.com

Please call or write for our free catalog. Our toll-free number to place an order or obtain a free catalog is 800-258-0929 or please use our regular business telephone 715-445-2214 for editorial comment and further information.

Library of Congress Catalog Number: 00-102691

ISBN: 0-87341-862-X

Printed in Canada

WINCHESTER is a trademark of Olin Corporation and is used y permission. Neither the author, the editor, nor the publisher e sponsored by or associated with the Olin Corporation.

WINCHESTER
RARITIES

TOM WEBSTE
EDITED BY DAVID D.

Table of Contents
Winchester Rarities

Introduction
Spotlight on Advertising

The book you're holding was not meant to be a history book. It's a picture book of rare items; the first book ever issued in color that focuses primarily on the beautiful and diverse advertising materials Winchester produced prior to 1935. But we hope you find important historical information in it, even if you're not an advertising collector. Pictures of shotshell boxes, for example, used in general advertising in a particular year help us all to catalog and document important label style changes.

Winchester history can be divided into several distinct eras. There's the pre-1900 Winchester, struggling to survive and then learning to thrive.

There's the era from 1900 to 1906 when the company was hammering out a corporate image it could live with for a long time. That struggle was dramatically reflected in "Winchester" logo typefaces that were all over the board from a design standpoint. Finally, someone decided to decide. Winchester launched the big red "W" in 1906, as well as the "lightning strike" logo, and has stayed with them ever since.

There's the period from 1906 to World War I. At the end of this era, in July 1917, the company launched

The Winchester Junior Rifle Corps. It wrapped patriotism and the bond between fathers and children, particularly sons, into one big package. It brought gun safety and shooting competitions to the attention of America's young people. That era ended when the National Rifle Association took over the WJRC program in 1924.

In the meantime, Winchester was already well into another era in company history. The 1920s. The roaring '20s for America. The growing '20s for Winchester.

The company bought every significant hardware, tool, knife, sporting goods, appliance and paint company in sight. Or so it seemed. They bought the Associated Simmons Hardware Company and its national chain of warehouses. They started "The Winchester Stores," many of them company-owned, but then later expanded the concept to a retailer network numbering more than 6,500 stores. This was Winchester's Golden Age.

In the first edition of the recently released *Standard Catalog of Winchester*, we described and priced every conceivable company product we could document or

Fishing Tackle - Point-of-Purchase display. Winchester produced very few POP displays for fishing tackle. Probably created in the 1923-1929 era. This is the only one like this ever found. Tabs on lower panel fit into slots to create a three-faced, curved back as a stand to place on the floor or in a window. Overall size is 42" wide x 30" high; tackle and lures panel is 29 1/2" wide x 8" high. From Tom Webster collection. Photo by D. Kowalski.

Values: $4,750 - $5,000.

Boy and Black Terrier. Window poster used in the 1918 advertising campaign materials. The boy holding his Model 90 and his sidekick, the black terrier, would become primary images used to promote the Winchester Junior Rifle Corps. Only two of these posters are known to exist. Image size is 17" wide x 35" high; overall size is 17 3/4" wide x 36" high. From Tom Webster collection. Photo by D. Kowalski.

Values: $5,000 - $6,000.

Boys! Use Winchester Baseball Goods - a two-sided counter sign displayed in Winchester Stores in 1920s. The company produced scores of these in three sizes. This sign shows the classic schoolyard method of choosing teams. The two captains grab the bat handle, alternating hand over hand; the one who ends up gripping the very top gets to pick the first player. The backside promotes Monkey Wrenches. Image size is 6 1/2" wide x 10" high. From Tom Webster collection. Photo by D. Kowalski.

Values: $700 - $800.

Red-haired Woman with Hat and Gun - metal sign. While we have not covered unauthorized "reproductions" in this volume, we show this light metal sign produced in the 1990s of a much-larger rare poster from 1914. We do not know who the manufacturer was but it was not Winchester. Winchester did try its hand at reproductions for a brief period in the 1960s. Company reproductions of these small metal signs typically had cardboard backer boards with the metal edges of the sign crimped around them. This sign is 7 1/8" wide x 16" high. From Tom Webster collection. Photo by D. Kowalski.

Values: $10 - $25
(metal reproductions).

"As Good As The Gun" - Winchester Store advertisement. This is an original poster on newsprint created by Winchester in the 1920s. The other side (front) has four scenes including wood chopping and the Winchester factory. Several hundred of these were reportedly discovered folded in a large wooden crate. That has led to speculation they were actually unauthorized "reproductions" flooding the market. There is also reportedly a one-sided "reproduction" being sold. From Tom Webster collection. Photo by D. Kowalski.

Values: $175 - $250
(original two-sided version).

photograph. You name it. Winchester probably made it or sold it in the 1920s.

When the 1920s ended, so did the old Winchester, for all practical purposes. It was hurtling toward bankruptcy, finding it was not immune to the general economic chaos that became known as The Great Depression. The Winchester Repeating Arms Company was reorganized in 1929, went into receivership in 1931, and was finally purchased by Western Cartridge Company in late 1931.

Western maintained a few of the old Winchester product lines from the 1920s. Winchester firearms and ammunition came back to center stage and continue to this day. Western supplied roller skates, flashlights and

batteries for several more decades. But the Winchester Stores were gone.

If you want a solid history book, we recommend *Winchester Repeating Arms Company; It's History and Development from 1865 to 1981*, by Herbert G. Houze. *The Standard Catalog of Winchester* also has a brief historical overview of the company. The "Winchester Shotshell Timeline" created just for the book has been especially helpful for all Winchester collectors trying to date various materials.

We have generally used the picture captions in this book to convey relevant historical information. And within each broad category, we have tried to present pieces in chronological order. There is still much we

Samples of brass and paper shotshells in a wood case. Winchester salesmen were given various sample cases to help sell company products. This rare and very early version probably dates from 1883 or 1884. Rival shells replaced the "Second Quality" ("S.Q.") line in 1884. It has been reported that the "S.Q." line was discontinued in 1881 but the appearance of both S.Q. and Rival shells in this case seems to indicate otherwise. Winchester probably included the S.Q. shells for comparison purposes to help launch both the Star and Rival empty brass shells in 1884. When closed, box measures 12 3/4" long x 6 1/2" wide x 3" high. From Tom Webster collection. Photo by D. Kowalski.

Values: $1,750 - $2,500.

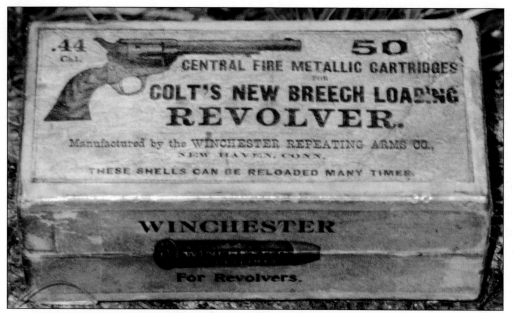

Cartridge Box - .44 caliber shells for Colt revolver. This extremely rare box pictures the Colt single-action Army revolver, as well as a side label with a headstamped shell. Dates from approximately 1880. It may be the only one in existence. From Ray T. Giles collection. Photo by R. Giles.

Values:
$10,000 - $15,000.

don't know about dating Winchester items. Because Winchester did not observe the practice of putting a copyright date on all its advertising we are now faced with making educated guesses about many items. If you have more information about pieces we've pictured, we welcome your input for possible future editions.

Winchester clearly understood the power of bold and colorful graphics. The editor of this volume, who has 20 year's of successful experience creating, selling and evaluating advertising for a variety of companies in a broad range of industries, has attempted to add his insights where appropriate.

We certainly have not ignored non-advertising collectibles in this issue. You will see some of the rarest of Winchester's non-advertising products in color. For example, you will find a full collection in color, in excellent to mint condition, of the 24 matched fishing plugs (eight colors in three styles) Winchester produced. We have included significant pieces from the Winchester Store era, as well as the Winchester Junior Rifle Corps.

We are indebted to the photo contributors to this volume. With their help and their photography, a wide audience is seeing many of the rarest Winchester collectibles for the first time. If your name is on a photo credit in this book, we thank you profusely. We're sure our readers will thank you.

The other unique aspect of this volume, as it was with the *Standard Catalog of Winchester*, is that we have priced these collectibles. In the Standard Catalog, we established definitions for grading in the major categories, then offered valuations in three or four grades of condition. Market pricing is always in a state of flux. As new editions of both these volumes are printed, we will update prices to reflect the current market. Input from readers will be appreciated and incorporated in future editions.

We particularly welcome photographs of new and rare pieces we may not have seen before.

In *Winchester Rarities*, we've confined values to a range of prices from Good to Excellent condition. Our contributors have been asked for their input on what they believed their collectibles were "worth." Our senior author, with 45 years of Winchester collecting experience, then made final valuations.

We don't expect everyone to agree on the values presented. "Worth" is that price to which a willing buyer and a willing seller agree. The Winchester collecting arena is like many others. Some collectors want all their pieces to have a high value. They may want pieces owned by anyone else to have low values. Some have suggested we put high prices on rare pieces because we know there are one or two determined collectors who might pay any price for certain items. But we're more interested in what the item will bring in the general marketplace after one or two key collectors have what they want. In general, we believe we have priced collectibles in this volume conservatively.

Many specialty areas exist in Winchester collecting, some more mature than others. We believe there is room for new collectors, perhaps spurred by what they see in these pages. And we hope all will be guided by our motto, "Do unto others as you would have them do unto you."

Now, without further delay ... Welcome to *Winchester Rarities!*

Tom E. Webster
David D. Kowalski
August, 2000

Winchester, Winchester-Western and Winchester Store Wall Calendars

While the Winchester Arms Company officially began in 1865, it would take some 22 years before they issued their first "corporate" poster-size wall calendar. This concept began in 1887 and would continue until 1934, with only two interruptions.

Winchester calendar collectors are interested in a span of 53 years from 1887 through 1934, during which Winchester produced 36 different poster-size wall calendars. If the math doesn't seem to work out, that's because Winchester did not offer any wall calendars from 1902 through 1911. There were no Winchester calendars offered in 1931 or 1932, years when the new owner, Western Cartridge Co., was getting the company reorganized and streamlined. Then combined Winchester/Western calendars were offered in 1933 and 1934. We present all of these full-size calendars.

We conclude the chapter with "Winchester Store" calendars from across the United States. They have become very desirable collectibles in the past decade. These were produced from 1921 through 1930, typically in smaller sizes than Winchester's corporate calendar. Styles are also diverse since Winchester retailers could use either the corporate scene from that year or, it appears, virtually any painting they chose. We present more than a dozen to give you a generous, but by no means complete, cross section of this category.

As a word of caution on calendars (and posters), I have always made it a practice to buy only those with the original metal bands that were crimped to the top and/or bottom. We will indicate the original band placement to help you spot authentic pieces.

Finally, we have also given overall re-measured sizes of actual calendars photographed (not simply repeated the sizes offered in other sources). Some calendars have a live matter area slightly smaller than the overall size (typical borders are 3/8 - 1/2"). Also keep in mind that paper trimming and metal band crimping 70 or 80 years ago was not a process that was identical, calendar after calendar.

1887 Calendar

1888 Calendar

Winchester put the corporate name on its first wall calendar some 22 years after its founding in July, 1865. This 1887 calendar is one of the rarest of the series; only about 8-10 of them have been discovered to date. It promotes the Model 1886 rifle, but also sets the precedent of using multiple scenes that was to continue until 1901. The artist is unknown. Overall size is 14 1/2" wide x 21 7/8" high. Metal bands top and bottom. From Curt Bowman collection. Photo by C. Bowman.

Values: $10,000 - $15,000.

Winchester's second calendar is the rarest of their poster-size wall calendars. Only three or four have been found to date. They used illustrations purchased from 1887 issues of Harper's Weekly magazine. Overall size is 14 5/8" wide x 21 7/8" high. Metal bands top and bottom. From Tom Webster collection. Photo by D. Kowalski.

Values: $10,000 - $15,000.

1889 Calendar

1890 Calendar

The 1889 edition launches another tradition used by many Winchester artists of putting titles on multiple calendar scenes. This one has scenes named "In Luck," "Just in the Nick of Time," and "Keep Low." Painted by A.B. Frost. The first of eight calendars Frost painted for Winchester. He also painted the calendar scenes for 1895-1901. Arthur Burdett Frost (1851-1928), one of the most popular illustrators of his day, often depicted American rural life. He is best known for his illustrations of the "Uncle Remus" stories by Joel Chandler Harris. This calendar not quite as rare as 1887 or 1888. Overall size is 14 5/8" wide x 22 3/4" high. Metal bands top and bottom. From Tom Webster collection. Photo by D. Kowalski.

Values: $9,000 - $12,000.

Multiple hunting scenes were also typical of the earliest calendars. This specimen also shows it got hung up and used; the December page is wrinkled and torn on the bottom left corner. Winchester used illustrations from 1883 and 1885 that they purchased from Harper's Weekly, the same source as the 1888 calendar. Also not quite as rare as 1887 or 1888. Overall size is 14 1/2" wide x 23 1/2" high. Metal bands top and bottom. From Tom Webster collection. Photo by D. Kowalski.

Values: $8,500 - $12,000.

1891 Calendar   1892 Calendar

Frederic Remington, painting his first Winchester calendar, adopts the concept of multiple hunting scenes. The circular scene has the caption, "Shoot or you'll lose him." Remington lived from 1861-1909. His more than 2700 paintings and drawings typically depict accurate and action-filled scenes from his life on the Western Plains. His calendars are sought by collectors of Frederic Remington art, by collectors of cowboy art and, of course, by Winchester collectors. Overall size is 14 5/8" wide x 23 3/4" high. Metal bands top and bottom. From Tom Webster collection. Photo by D. Kowalski.

Values: $7,500 - $10,000.

Frederic Remington's second Winchester calendar includes a new group of target species and habitats. But he again includes one of his favorite images, the mounted horseman. Another very collectible Remington calendar, as they all are. Overall size is 14 3/4" wide x 23 1/2" high. Metal bands top and bottom. From Tom Webster collection. Photo by D. Kowalski.

Values: $7,500 - $10,000.

1893 Calendar

1894 Calendar

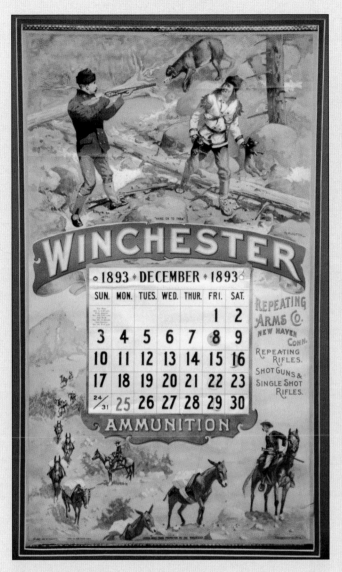

The Indian guide is advised, "Hang on to them," as he carries off the bear cubs. Painted by Frederic Remington, his third successive calendar. Remington also shows a mule train "Protected by the Winchester." Overall size is 14 1/2" wide x 24 3/4" high. Metal bands top and bottom. From Tom Webster collection. Photo by D. Kowalski.

Values: $7,500 - $10,000.

"Ranchmen protecting Stock from Wolves" is the major scene at top. "A Surprise Party" is the bottom scene. Painted by Frederic Remington, the fourth and last of his calendar efforts for Winchester. All of the Frederic Remington calendars have increased in value through the years and that trend is expected to continue. Overall size is 14 3/8" wide x 26 7/8" high. Metal bands top and bottom. From Tom Webster collection. Photo by D. Kowalski.

Values: $7,500 - $10,000.

1895 Calendar

1896 Calendar

"Success" is the top scene; it was also used as the central scene on the "Double W" cartridge board of 1897-1898. "An Unexpected Change," is the bottom scene. Painted by A.B. Frost. Frost's first calendar for Winchester was 1889. This is his second Winchester calendar and the first in a series of seven straight years that he painted their calendar scene. Frost's first calendar (1889) brings high prices but the last seven are not even close to its value. Overall size is 14 3/8" wide x 26 1/4" high. Metal bands top and bottom. From Tom Webster collection. Photo by D. Kowalski.

Values: $1,400 - $1,750.

"The Finishing Shot" is the caption for the top scene. A.B. Frost, in his third calendar, again uses a north woods setting for the major scene; this time his hunters are facing a wounded moose. The other two scenes are not captioned. Overall size is 14" wide x 26 1/2" high. Metal bands top and bottom. From Tom Webster collection. Photo by D. Kowalski.

Values: $1,200 - $1,500.

1897 Calendar

1898 Calendar

"A Chance Shot" is the caption for the top scene. Here A.B. Frost, in his fourth Winchester calendar, creates a horse-and-cowboy scene very reminiscent of the prior work of Frederic Remington. "An Interrupted Dinner" is the bottom scene. Overall size is 14 1/4" wide x 26 3/8" high. Metal bands top and bottom. From Tom Webster collection. Photo by D. Kowalski.

Values: $1,200 - $1,500.

"The 30 Did It" is the caption for the top scene; with A.B. Frost coming back to a woodland setting for elk hunting. The duck-hunting scene at bottom is not captioned and is the only waterfowl scene on his Winchester calendars. This particular calendar also has overprinted identification of the Stark & Weckesser retail store in Dayton, Ohio. We're not sure if retailers could request this identification from Winchester's corporate printer or the retailer would have enlisted a local printer to customize his calendars. This fifth Frost calendar shows another drop in values. Overall size is 14 3/8" wide x 26 1/2" high. Metal bands top and bottom. From Tom Webster collection. Photo by D. Kowalski.

Values: $900 - $1,200.

1899 Calendar

1900 Calendar

The bear hunters agree "We've Got Him Sure" in the top scene; "Snipe Shooting" is the bottom scene. Painted by A.B. Frost. The sixth Frost calendar. As an aside, the company continues to experiment with its "Winchester" logo typeface, coming back to a "serif" typeface after one year of a block-lettered "sans serif" version. Overall size is 14 1/4" wide x 26 3/8" high. Metal bands top and bottom. From Tom Webster collection. Photo by D. Kowalski.

Values: $900 - $1,200.

"Waiting for a Shot at the Old Ram" is the caption for the top scene; "Quail Shooting" is the bottom scene. The seventh calendar painted by A.B. Frost. The "Winchester" logo now gets "fancier" with a very ornate "W" with a long "tail." Overall size is 14 3/8" wide x 26 1/4" high. Metal bands top and bottom. From Tom Webster collection. Photo by D. Kowalski.

Values: $900 - $1,200.

1901 Calendar

1912 Calendar

"Fresh Meat for the Outfit" is the top scene; "Winter Fun on the Farm" is bottom scene. A.B. Frost's eighth (and last) calendar is unique for several reasons. It's the last Winchester calendar with multiple scenes and the last one offered for a decade. The 1901 issue is fairly rare and valued higher than the previous three. Overall size is 14 1/4" wide x 26 3/4" high. Metal bands top and bottom. From Tom Webster collection. Photo by D. Kowalski.

Values: $1,200 - $1,500.

Winchester calendars come roaring back with a larger size, bolder graphics and the "lightning strike" typeface for the "Winchester" logo they created in 1906 and generally adopted on all packaging by 1910. This new logo typeface would be used on all future Winchester calendars, as well as a single dominant and dramatic scene or image. Painted by N.C. Wyeth. Overall size is 15" wide x 29 3/4" high. Metal bands top and bottom. From Tom Webster collection. Photo by D. Kowalski.

Values: $2,700 - $3,000.

1913 Calendar

1914 Calendar

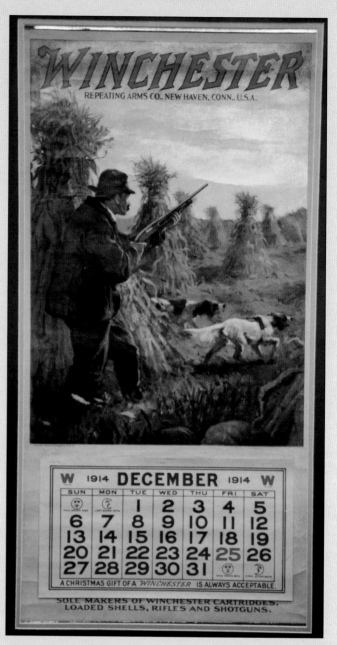

The rather endearing, pipe-smoking hunter with the white goatee is carrying the first Model 12. This has created additional demand for this calendar among Model 12 aficionados. Painted by Robert B. Robinson, who lived from 1886-1952. Overall size is 15 1/4" wide x 29 1/2" high. Metal bands top and bottom. From Tom Webster collection. Photo by D. Kowalski.

Values: $2,700 - $3,000.

The first post – 1912 Winchester calendar depicting an upland game hunting scene. This calendar painting has been attributed incorrectly in the past to Philip R. Goodwin. Overall size is 15" wide x 29 3/4" high. Metal bands top and bottom. From Tom Webster collection. Photo by D. Kowalski.

Values: $1,400 - $1,700.

1915 Calendar

A female mountain goat is protecting her kid from a golden eagle. Painted by Lynn Bogue Hunt (1878-1960), a noted wildlife artist especially famous for his duck paintings. He also painted several of the larger Winchester advertising displays. This was the first calendar he painted for Winchester. He didn't do the second one until 1929. Overall size is 15" wide x 30" high. Metal bands top and bottom. From Tom Webster collection. Photo by D. Kowalski.

Values: $1,500 - $1,700.

1916 Calendar

Two hunters on a mountain ledge with their Airedale terrier. Winchester turned to Philip R. Goodwin for this painting. Goodwin (1882-1935) was commissioned for several paintings by Winchester and also by many other ammunition and outdoor-related companies of the day. His reputation endures and his work is still pursued even by non-Winchester collectors who admire his realistic, dramatic art. Overall size is 15" wide x 29 3/4" high. Metal band on top. From Tom Webster collection. Photo by D. Kowalski.

Values: $1,700 - $2,000.

1917 Calendar

1918 Calendar

This action-packed calendar is highly sought after by both Winchester and Western cowboy art collectors, which has driven up the price. Painted by W.K. Leigh (1866-1955), who continues to be a highly regarded Western artist. Overall size is 14 7/8" wide x 29 3/4" high. Metal band on top. From Tom Webster collection. Photo by D. Kowalski.

Values: $3,700 - $4,000.

Dad offers pointers to his son on how to stop the running rabbit. Different versions of this scene were also used on other Winchester posters and advertising, including a poster released for the 1918 advertising campaign, as well as to promote their newly created Winchester Junior Rifle Corps. Winchester believed the image "makes a strong appeal to both father and son." Painted by George Brehm (1878-1966). Overall size is 19 3/4" wide x 39 1/4" high. Metal band on top. From Tom Webster collection. Photo by D. Kowalski.

Values: $1,400 - $1,700.

1919 Calendar

1920 Calendar

A farmer stops his plow horses long enough to gaze at a cloud pattern that appears to recreate the American flag. However, the patriotic theme hasn't particularly excited Winchester collectors about this calendar. Painted by Robert Amick (1879-1969), reportedly born in a log cabin in Colorado but graduated from Yale Law School, who practiced law for two years before he turned to painting. Overall size is 19" wide x 38 3/8" high. Metal band on top. From Tom Webster collection. Photo by D. Kowalski.

Values: $1,400 - $1,700.

Another father-and-son hunting theme, this one a more subtle tie-in to the company's Winchester Junior Rifle Corps concept. Painter is unknown. This calendar also shows one of the many perils of earlier incorrect storage ... horizontal wrinkles from having been stored rolled but still getting creased. Overall size is 19 3/4" wide x 38 3/4" high. Metal band on top. From Tom Webster collection. Photo by D. Kowalski.

Values: $1,400 - $1,700.

1921 Calendar

1922 Calendar

The third calendar in four years (and the last one) Winchester produced with the father-and-son theme. This father and son are hunting pheasant or quail in an upland setting. Painted by Arthur Fuller (1889-1966), best known as a frequent illustrator for Field and Stream. Overall size is 14 1/4" wide x 25 1/2" high. Metal band on top. From Tom Webster collection. Photo by D. Kowalski.

Values: $1,400 - $1,700.

This imposing grizzly bear blocking the way on a mountain ledge has given both horse and rider a rush of adrenaline. Collectors of cowboy art have also helped drive up the price of this calendar. Painted by H.C. Edwards (1868-1922) in the last few years of his life. Overall size is 14 5/8" wide x 26 1/8" high. Metal band on top. From Tom Webster collection. Photo by D. Kowalski.

Values: $2,700 - $3,000.

1923 Calendar

1924 Calendar

The hunter on a rock outcrop stalks bighorn sheep. Painted by Philip R. Goodwin, his second one for Winchester. He also did the illustrations for Jack London's original edition of the "Call of the Wild." Overall size is 13 3/4" wide x 25 7/8" high. Metal band on top. From Tom Webster collection. Photo by D. Kowalski.

Values: $1,700 - $2,000.

The duck hunter is holding a Model 12, making this edition fairly popular with Model 12 collectors. However, this otherwise nondescript painting has equally "unexciting" values. Painted by G. Ryder. Overall size is 13 5/8" wide x 27 1/8" high. Metal band on top. From Tom Webster collection. Photo by D. Kowalski.

Values: $1,200 - $1,500.

1925 Calendar

1926 Calendar

These were reportedly bear dogs belonging to some member of the Winchester family. Two redbone hounds are in background. Painted by Henry Rankin Poore (1858-1940). Values jump back up for this popular calendar. The same painting was also offered to stores in a wide wood frame (then later as a print that only pictured the frame) for display purposes. Also note that this calendar was both wider and significantly shorter than either the 1924 or 1926 versions. Overall size is 15 1/4" wide x 21 1/8" high. Metal bands on top and bottom. From Tom Webster collection. Photo by D. Kowalski.

Values: $2,700 - $3,000.

Goodwin's hunter is again wearing his red bandana (as he was in the 1923 calendar). The Grizzly Bear obviously means business in this dramatic scene. The third and last Winchester calendar painted by Philip R. Goodwin is also his most valuable one. Overall size is 14 5/8" wide x 26 1/4" high. Metal band on top. From Tom Webster collection. Photo by D. Kowalski.

Values: $2,700 - $3,000.

1927 Calendar

1928 Calendar

The hunter on snowshoes gets ready to shoot by pulling off his glove with his teeth when he sees the big buck and the doe. Painted by Frank Stick (1884-1966). This man on snowshoes should not be mistaken for Philip R. Goodwin's 1906 poster of a hunter on snowshoes facing a wolf pack. Overall size is 14 3/4" wide x 26 1/4" high. Metal bands on top and bottom. From Tom Webster collection. Photo by D. Kowalski.

Values: $1,400 - $1,700.

The moose hunter standing in canoe behind the boulder peeks carefully at his quarry. This calendar is both more rare than the 1927 issue and also considered more artistically desirable by many veteran Winchester collectors. Painted by R. Farrington Elwell (1874-1962), who managed "Buffalo Bill" Cody's Wyoming ranch from 1896-1921. Overall size is 14 3/4" wide x 26 3/8" high. Metal bands on top and bottom. From Tom Webster collection. Photo by D. Kowalski.

Values: $2,200 - $2,500.

1929 Calendar

1930 Calendar

A trio of ring-necked pheasants flushed by dog and hunter. Painted by Lynn Bogue Hunt, who also painted the 1915 Winchester calendar, as well as many scenes for other Winchester advertising material. Overall size is 14 3/4" wide x 26" high. Metal bands on top and bottom. From Tom Webster collection. Photo by D. Kowalski.

Values: $1,500 - $1,800.

The most unique aspect of this Winchester "Mountain Man" calendar is that six different outdoor or product scenes were used for every new group of two monthly pages (see the next five photographs). This photograph of the full calendar has the March/April page turned out featuring two fishermen playing a bass. Painter is unknown. Overall size is 14 7/8" wide x 25 1/4" high. The center panel of each calendar page scene measures 9 7/8" wide x 7 3/8" high. Metal band on top. From Tom Webster collection. Photo by D. Kowalski.

Values: $700 - $1,000.

Winchester used the "Mountain Man" image heavily and his collectibility has suffered a bit as a result. The painter of the "Mountain Man" is unknown, perhaps an indication that this calendar was being produced as economically as possible by a company on the verge of bankruptcy. This was also the last Winchester calendar for two years, none being produced in 1931 or 1932 with the "Winchester" name while the new owner, Western Cartridge Co., was reorganizing Winchester.

1930 Calendar. July/August page shines the spotlight on flashlights and batteries. From Curt Bowman collection. Photo by C. Bowman.

1930 Calendar. January/February page combines a household appliance and cutlery scene next to a workshop and tool scene. From Curt Bowman collection. Photo by C. Bowman.

1930 Calendar. September/October page pictures a flight of ducks and promotes Winchester's Model 12 and Model 97 shotguns, as well as shotshells. Painted by Lynn Bogue Hunt. From Curt Bowman collection. Photo by C. Bowman.

1930 Calendar. November/December "big buck" scene promotes Winchester rifles and cartridges. Painted by Lynn Bogue Hunt. From Curt Bowman collection. Photo by C. Bowman.

1930 Calendar. May/June page promotes roller skating, roller skates and ice skates. From Curt Bowman collection. Photo by C. Bowman.

1933 Calendar

1934 Calendar

The 1933 Winchester/Western Calendar scene inside the hunting shack was painted by William Eaton, born in 1861. Among the lowest values for a Winchester calendar. Overall size is 14 7/8" wide x 27 1/2" high. Metal band on top. From Tom Webster collection. Photo by D. Kowalski.

Values: $700 - $900.

On the 1934 Winchester/Western Calendar, a young slingshot-toting hunter is thinking, "I wish I had Dad's Winchester." This appealing young boy was a powerful image for Winchester/Western and this calendar remains a popular one. Painted by Eugene Iverd (1893-1938). Overall size is 14 7/8" wide x 27 7/8" high. Metal band on top. From Tom Webster collection. Photo by D. Kowalski.

Values: $1,200 - $1,400.

1921 Winchester Store Calendar

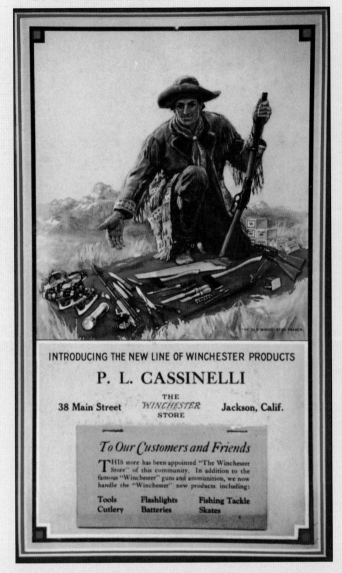

"The Old Winchester Trader" displays his assortment of guns, ammunition, tools and sporting goods. Calendar produced by P.L. Casinelli, Jackson, California. Overall size is 7 3/4" wide x 13 3/4" high. From Tom Webster collection. Photo by D. Kowalski.

Values: $700 - $900.

1922 Winchester Store Calendar

This is a smaller version of the 1922 corporate calendar. Painted by H.C. Edwards. Calendar for Davis Hardware Store, Chester Depot, Vermont. Overall size is 10" wide x 19 1/4" high. From Tom Webster collection. Photo by D. Kowalski.

Values: $1,200 - $1,500.

1922 Winchester Store Calendar   1922 Winchester Store Calendar

A radiant young woman graces this calendar for Royal Hardware Co., Royalton, Illinois. They offer "Hardware, Furniture, Harness, Cutlery, Sporting Goods, and Painters' Supplies." Overall size is 11 3/4" wide x 16 1/8" high. From Tom Webster collection. Photo by D. Kowalski.

Values: $500 - $700.

"The Prize Herd" of Guernsey dairy cattle stands in a farm pond. Calendar for H.R. Ritter, Grinnell, Iowa. Overall size is 8 3/8" wide x 15 1/2" high. From Tom Webster collection. Photo by D. Kowalski.

Values: $500 - $700.

1923 Winchester Store Calendar

1924 Winchester Store Calendar

The Philip R. Goodwin painting from the 1923 corporate calendar was used by Halladay's Store, Hillsboro, New Hampshire. Philip R. Goodwin adds value to virtually every collectible showing his work. Overall size is 9 7/8" wide x 19 1/8" high. From Tom Webster collection. Photo by D. Kowalski.

Values: $1,000 - $1,200.

Here is another calendar using the corporate painting for the year done by G. Ryder. And like its larger 1924 counterpart, this rather drab duck hunting scene has not generally grabbed the attention of collectors, unless they're fans of the Model 12. Created for P.A. Krause & Sons, Fullerton, Nebraska. Overall size is 9 7/8" wide x 19 1/2" high. From Tom Webster collection. Photo by D. Kowalski.

Values: $600 - $800.

1924 Winchester Store Calendar

1925 Winchester Store Calendar

This calendar (missing the January page) has a new full scene for every month. Succeeding pages develop the theme of "From Forest to Home Panorama" showing logs cut from the forest, moving down river to the mill to produce lumber and various wood products. Produced by Schmid & Lehrer Co., the Winchester Store in Springfield, Minnesota. Overall size of each page is 17 1/2" wide x 23 3/8" high. Values given for this calendar are with all 12 pages. From Tom Webster collection. Photo by D. Kowalski.

Values: $1,500 - $1,800.

The H. R. Poore painting of the bear dogs from the 1925 corporate calendar was the choice of the Smith-Palmiter Hardware Co., Inc., Sherburne, New York. Overall size is 11 7/8" wide x 18" high. From Tom Webster collection. Photo by D. Kowalski.

Values: $1,250 - $1,500.

1925 Winchester Store Calendar

1925 Winchester Store Calendar

"Doe-Wah-Jack Brings a Message of Good Cheer" was presented by A. Gillen, the Winchester Store in Lexington, Missouri. The Indian character, Doe Wah-Jack, also appeared on other calendars sponsored by the Round Oak Stove Company. The lower right emblem contains the additional promise that "The Round Oak Folks Make Good Goods Only." Overall size is 10 5/8" wide x 20 5/8" high. From Tom Webster collection. Photo by D. Kowalski.

Values: $1,250 - $1,500.

"Dream Light" by the famous artist Maxfield Parrish was chosen for this calendar from the A.S. Burchard Co. (city and state unknown). Edison Mazda Lamps was also a sponsor of the calendar. Overall size is 8 1/4" wide x 18 7/8" high. From Tom Webster collection. Photo by D. Kowalski.

Values: $1,250 - $1,500.

1926 Winchester Store Calendar

1926 Winchester Store Calendar

G.E. Morgan of Atkinson, Nebraska chose another unique format for this calendar that used a monthly page with a storage pocket and a tab at the bottom. They called it a "System Calendar" and also chose not to use a dominant visual image. Overall size is 10 3/8" wide x 13 5/8" high. From Tom Webster collection. Photo by D. Kowalski.

Values: $400 - $500.

Philip R. Goodwin painted this scene that also appeared on the large 1926 Winchester corporate calendar. Offered to customers by P.A. Krause & Sons, the Winchester Store in Fullerton, Nebraska. This calendar also has all individual month pages removed, leaving only the recap page with all months displayed. Overall size is 9 7/8" wide x 20 1/4" high. From Tom Webster collection. Photo by D. Kowalski.

Values: $1,250 - $1,500.

1927 Winchester Store Calendar

1928 Winchester Store Calendar

Wentworth Mercantile Co., the Winchester Store in Unionville, Missouri, used Frank Stick's deer hunter on snowshoes from the 1927 corporate calendar. Overall size is 9 7/8" wide x 20 5/8" high. From Tom Webster collection. Photo by D. Kowalski.

Values: $500 - $700.

A scene entitled "Protection" tops this calendar offered, apparently, by one of the Winchester-Simmons distribution centers. These Winchester-Simmons versions are much rarer than those offered by an individual Winchester Store. Overall size is 9 3/4" wide x 20 3/8" high. From Tom Webster collection. Photo by D. Kowalski.

Values: $500 - $700 (Winchester Store version); $1,200 - $1,500 (Winchester-Simmons version).

1929 Winchester Store Calendar

1930 Winchester Store Calendar

A Pony Express rider waves goodbye to a frontier couple. This scene was also used on one of Winchester's five-panel advertising sets from the late 1920s. Another example from the Winchester Store of P.A. Krause & Sons, Fullerton, Nebraska. Overall size is 9 3/4" wide x 20" high. From Tom Webster collection. Photo by D. Kowalski.

Values: $500 - $700.

Calendars from 1930 were probably the last ones offered by any Winchester Store. "Where Shelter Awaits" is the winter scene on this one painted by W.M. Thompson and used by the A.J.H. McNeill Hardware Store in Monticello, Iowa. Here's another individual calendar that was never used and still has the calendar page "Season's Greetings" cover flap intact. Overall size is 8 5/8" wide x 16 5/8" high. From Tom Webster collection. Photo by D. Kowalski.

Values: $500 - $700.

1929 Winchester Store Calendar

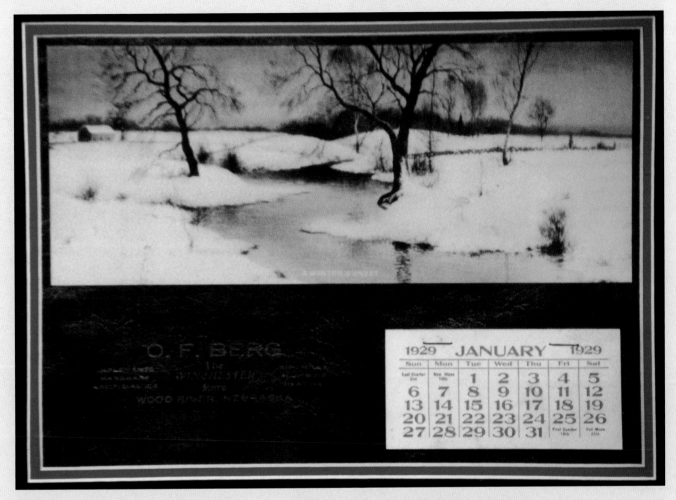

While most Winchester calendars have a vertical format, this one exhibits a rare horizontal format. It was produced by O.F. Berg, the Winchester Store in Wood River, Nebraska. The scene is entitled "A Winter Sunset." Overall size is 10 1/8" wide x 7" high. From Tom Webster collection. Photo by D. Kowalski.

Values: $500 - $700.

Wall Posters and Banners

During the period 1902 through 1911, Winchester stopped producing large wall calendars but they didn't abandon the wall-sized advertising concept. It actually took them the better part of three years to replace the wall calendar of 1901 with a set of advertising posters, the first in a long series.

The first two posters were offered in 1904; one promoted shotguns and shotshells (flying mallards) and its counterpart spotlighted rifles and cartridges (hunter on rock ledge with bighorn ram). These two pioneering efforts were then followed by a veritable flood of stunning wildlife posters, especially from 1905 through 1911. But Winchester would continue to produce posters and "hangers" for walls and store windows until 1930.

There are also some very striking and rare large banners that we present at the end of the chapter, as well as some classic pieces that appeared in both poster and sign versions.

Woman in the Saddle (Poster)

Woman in the Saddle. One of rarest posters. Perhaps only two still exist. It's likely they were only produced in this Spanish version. (We include examples of the same image seen on a firearms and cartridge booklet, as well as envelope, both only seen to date in Spanish.) It's also likely Winchester released all these items together in the same era of 1912-1914. The woman is holding a Model 92 carbine. The artist is unknown but some collectors speculate it was Frank Tenney Johnson. Overall size is 14 1/2" wide x 27 1/4" high. Metal bands top and bottom. From Joan Webster collection. Photo by T. Webster.

Values: $10,000 - $15,000 (Spanish).

Woman in the Saddle (Envelope)

Woman in the Saddle Envelope. One of the rarest envelopes, only found in a Spanish version. This one was postmarked in Puerto Rico but the year is unreadable. Overall size is 6 1/2" wide x 3 5/8" high. From Tom Webster collection. Photo by D. Kowalski.

Values: $600 - $700 (Spanish).

Woman Standing with Hat and Rifle

Woman Standing with Hat and Rifle. Another rare poster with about four examples known in English and two or three in Spanish. The model for this poster is the same as the "Woman in the Saddle" poster. Some collectors speculate the artist was Frank Tenney Johnson, who also painted posters for Colt as well as Hopkins and Allen. Very likely produced in the 1912-1914 era. Overall size is 14" wide x 41 1/2" high. Metal bands top and bottom. From George Cross collection. Photo by G. Cross.

Values: $8,000 - $10,000
(Spanish or English version).

Woman in the Saddle (Booklet)

Woman in the Saddle Booklet. Only produced for the Spanish market, we believe. Copyright date is not in booklet but it does show the Model 12 (first produced in 1912) as the newest gun offered by Winchester. The booklet contains 80 pages, plus the covers. Overall size is 8 3/4" wide x 5 1/2" high. From Tom Webster collection. Photo by D. Kowalski.

Values: $500 - $600 (Spanish).

Woman by Canoe

Cock of the Woods

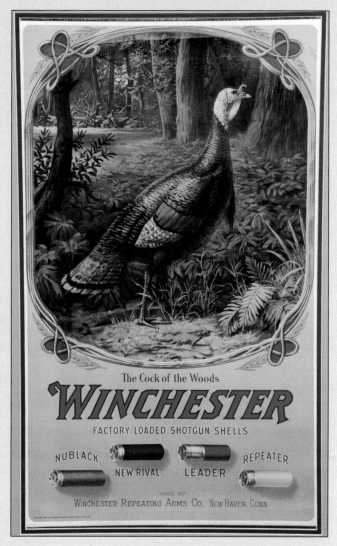

Woman by the Canoe. One of the rarest Winchester posters with perhaps only two copies known. Promotes .22 caliber automatic rifles. Copyright date is 1909. We have also seen examples of Winchester magazine advertising from 1909 using the same image. Artist unknown. Overall size is 10 3/4" wide x 20" high. Metal bands top and bottom. From Tom Webster collection. Photo by D. Kowalski.

Values: $9,000 -12,000.

The Cock of the Woods. The lifelike accuracy and stunning color of this work by an unknown artist makes this one of the most recognizable and sought after of all Winchester posters. Fortunately for collectors, it is not uncommon. Promotes Nublack, New Rival, Leader and Repeater loaded shotshells. Has 1905 copyright date. (Note both the "Winchester" logo similarities and the picture framed inside a woven oval, much like the following two posters from 1904.) Overall size is 14 7/8" wide x 24 7/8" high. Metal bands top and bottom. From Tom Webster collection. Photo by D. Kowalski.

Values: $6,500 - $9,000.

Hunter Standing over Big Horn Sheep

Three Mallard Ducks Flying

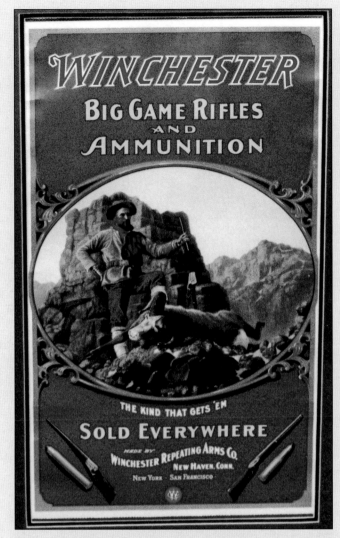

Hunter Standing over Fallen Big Horn Sheep. Companion to the "Mallards Flying" poster, this one promoting big game rifles and ammunition: "The Kind That Gets 'Em." Has 1904 copyright date. "Winchester" logo very similar to the one on the "Cock of the Woods" poster from 1905, both precursors of the "lightning strike" logo (especially evident on the "W") which Winchester started using in 1906 and generally adopted across the board by 1910. Poster size slightly smaller than typical later poster. Overall size is 15 1/8" wide x 25 7/8" high. Metal bands top and bottom. From Tom Webster collection. Photo by D. Kowalski.

Values: $3,400 - $3,700.

Three Mallard Ducks Flying. One of the first two posters, this one promotes factory loaded shotgun shells: "They Are Hitters." Has 1904 copyright date. (Another example of logo typeface experimentation leading up to the "lightning strike" logo. This logo differs from the one on the previous two posters only in the "W" which is now the so-called "devil's tail W" which, in turn, was resurrected briefly on some packaging in the late teens or early '20s. The "rebirth" of such images, including using these three ducks a decade later, often make accurate dating a real challenge.) Overall size is 14 3/4" wide x 25 1/4" high. Metal bands top and bottom. From Tom Webster collection. Photo by D. Kowalski.

Values: $3,400 - $3,700.

Man on Snowshoes with Wolf Pack

Man on Piebald Horse on Mountain

Man on Snowshoes with Wolf Pack. Tells a story in the snow (although we now know there has not been a documented case of a wolf pack attacking and killing a human). The first of five Winchester posters (we know of) painted by Philip R. Goodwin, this one from 1906. This poster was done the year following the "Cock of the Woods" and shows the full-blown "lightning strike" logo that Winchester will henceforth use on all products. (Don't mistake this work for Frank Stick's 1927 calendar painting.) Image size is 14 3/8" wide x 27 3/8" high; overall size is 15 1/2" wide x 29" high. Metal bands top and bottom. From Tom Webster collection. Photo by D. Kowalski.

Values: $4,000 - $4,500.

Man on Piebald Horse on Mountain. Philip R. Goodwin's second Winchester poster, this one from 1907. Goodwin's rider was apparently meant to resemble Teddy Roosevelt. Overall size is 15 1/4" wide x 29 1/8" high. Metal bands top and bottom. From Tom Webster collection. Photo by D. Kowalski.

Values: $1,700 - $2,200.

Grizzly Bear Coming Out of Cabin

Two Hunters Lying on Rock

Grizzly Bear Coming Out of Cabin. The surprised cabin owner is carrying his .401 caliber rifle. One of the most famous and desirable Philip R. Goodwin posters, released in 1909. Image size is 14 3/4" wide x 29 3/8" high; overall size is 15 1/4" wide x 29 1/2" high. Metal bands top and bottom. From Tom Webster collection. Photo by D. Kowalski.

Values: $4,000 - $4,500.

Two Hunters Lying on Rock, taking aim at Mountain Goats. This is Philip R. Goodwin's fourth poster for Winchester and one of his most sought-after posters. Has 1911 copyright date and now displays the Winchester big red "W" adopted in 1906. Overall size is 15" wide x 30" high. Metal bands top and bottom. From Tom Webster collection. Photo by D. Kowalski.

Values: $4,000 - $4,500.

Four Deer Going Up Snowy Mountainside

Four Deer Going Up Snowy Mountainside. The fifth poster painting by Philip R. Goodwin. The lack of significant detail and the fact these are mule deer make this the least sought after poster by Goodwin. Copyright date is 1912. Image size is 16" wide x 29 1/8" high; overall size is 16 1/2" wide x 29 3/4" high. Metal bands top and bottom. From Tom Webster collection. Photo by D. Kowalski.

Values: $1,500 - $2,000.

Woman in Yellow Hunting Coat

Woman in Yellow Hunting Coat with Setter Dog. Winchester uses another image of a woman hunter in this 1912 poster. Overall size is 14 5/8" wide x 30" high. Metal bands top and bottom. From Tom Webster collection. Photo by D. Kowalski.

Values: $3,700 - $4,000.

Woman in Hunting Coat (now red). Winchester re-colors the woman hunter for cover of their "Winchester Record" of June 4, 1920. From Tim Melcher collection. Photo by TIM.

Eight Canada Geese Flying

Chesapeake Retrieving Canvasback Duck

Eight Canada Geese Flying. This poster, with a copyright line of 1907, is the first in a series of four we believe were probably issued within a year or two of each other. This one promotes factory loaded shells and repeating shotguns. Artist unknown. Image size is 15" wide x 28 1/2" high; overall size is 15 1/2" wide x 29 1/8" high. Metal bands top and bottom. From Tom Webster collection. Photo by D. Kowalski.

Values: $2,200 - $2,700.

Chesapeake Bay Retriever retrieving Canvasback Duck. Promotes self-loading shotguns. Like the poster before it and the two that follow, this one displays the "lightning strike" logo first used in 1906 but does not show the big red "W" that also was adopted in late 1906. Artist unknown. Overall size is 15 1/2" wide x 26" high. Metal bands top and bottom. From Tom Webster collection. Photo by D. Kowalski.

Values: $2,700 - $3,000.

Setter and Pointer - 20 Gauge

Pointer and Setter - Repeating Shotguns

Setter and Pointer - promoting 20 gauge Shotguns. This poster and the companion one that follows are also probably from the 1906-1907 era. Advertising that promotes 20 gauge guns would tend to be valued higher than a generic piece or one about 12 gauge models. Artist unknown. Image size is 15 7/8" wide x 29 1/4" high; overall size is 16 1/4" wide x 30" high. Metal bands top and bottom. From Tom Webster collection. Photo by D. Kowalski.

Values: $1,500 - $1,700.

Pointer and Setter - promoting Repeating Shotguns. This is clearly the companion piece to the prior "20 Gauge" poster. Here the English pointer is in the foreground and the "feather-tailed" setter is in the background. Artist unknown. Image size is 15 7/8" wide x 29 1/2" high; overall size is 16 1/4" wide x 30 1/4" high. Metal bands top and bottom. From Tom Webster collection. Photo by D. Kowalski.

Values: $1,100 - $1,400.

Pointer and Setter (Dupont Powder)

Pointer and Setter (Dupont Powder). Small cardboard poster (no easel on back) - "The Hunter's Inspiration" - has 1903 copyright. Dupont Powder (a Winchester supplier) apparently printed "Winchester Shot Shells" on bottom margin and used as consumer giveaway to help market Winchester shells. Back reads: "Dupont Smokeless again wins the highest average for the year. Fred Gilbert, shooting Dupont Powder, stands at the head of the list. A remarkable record for man and powder. E.I. Dupont deNemours & Company, Wilmington, Delaware. Established 1802." Edmund H. Osthaus (1858-1928) was reportedly the artist. Image size is 12 3/8" wide x 7 3/4" high; overall size is 12 5/8" wide x 8 1/8" high. From Tom Webster collection. Photo by D. Kowalski.

Values: $400 - $600.

Shoot Them and Avoid Trouble - "Framed"

Shoot Them And Avoid Trouble. This highly controversial original poster included the frame-like border around the image area. Released to stores in 1908, the ambiguous interpretation of the "Shoot Them" advice caused Winchester to recall the posters and trim off the outside "frame" portion. They would also re-issue the image portion only in 1936. Overall area (including "frame" border) measures 32 5/8" wide x 24 5/8" high. From Tom Webster collection. Photo by D. Kowalski.

Values: $3,500 - $5,000 (Original version).

Two Setters - Small Poster

Two Grouse Flying

Two Setters - small poster. Probably another consumer free giveaway issued before 1910. Uses the new "lightning strike" logo but the big "W" is not used. We also include the small label on the back. Artist unknown. Image size is 8" wide x 11" high. From Tom Webster collection. Photo by D. Kowalski.

Values: $400 - $500.

What the name "Winchester" means

The Winchester Company is the greatest organization of its kind in the world. It makes a gun that cannot be duplicated by any other manufacturer.

No Winchester barrel varies one one-thousandth of an inch from a straight line, or one one-thousandth of an inch in thickness or diameter.

Every gun or rifle that bears the name "Winchester" is fired over fifty times with excess loads for strength, smooth action and accuracy.

All Winchester barrels are finished by the Bennett Process, which gives the barrel a finish that lasts a lifetime; hard to scratch and resists rust.

This care in manufacturing explains why more Winchesters are used by expert shooters than all other small arms combined.

Write for the Winchester Catalog

Winchester Repeating Arms Company
Dept. 34   New Haven, Conn.

Two Grouse Flying. Promotes Model 97 shotgun. Copyright 1909. Another instance where Winchester uses new "lightning strike" logo but not the big red "W" introduced at least two years earlier. Artist is Edward Knoble. Image size is 14 1/2" wide x 29 1/2" high; overall size is 15" wide x 30 1/2" high. From Tom Webster collection. Photo by D. Kowalski.

Values: $1,800 - $2,500.

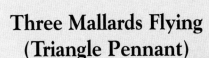

Three Mallards Flying (Triangle Pennant)

Three Mallards Flying - two-sided triangular pennant. The same scene and copy on both sides. Same mallard trio that appeared on 1904 poster. Pennant probably used as both store sign and consumer giveaway. Only one known to have survived. Overall size is 18" long (from center of base to tip) x 6" high. Light cardboard. From Tom Webster collection. Photo by D. Kowalski.

Values: $2,500 - $2,750.

Mountain Lion (Long Poster) & Three Mallards Flying (Long Poster)

LEFT: Mountain Lion - long poster. While the "Mallards Flying" companion poster promoted shotguns and shells, this one advertised cartridges and rifles. Painted by Lynn Bogue Hunt. The only one ever found. Overall size is 10 3/8" wide x 59 5/8" high. From Tom Webster collection. Photo by D. Kowalski.

Values: $3,250 - $3,500.

RIGHT: Three Mallards Flying - long poster. Companion to Mountain Lion long poster. General dimensions and vertical length make these a very unusual format for Winchester. Painted by Lynn Bogue Hunt. The only one ever found. Overall size is 10 3/8" wide x 59 5/8" high. From Tom Webster collection. Photo by D. Kowalski.

Values: $3,250 - $3,500.

Mr. and Mrs. Adolph Topperwein

Seven Shooting Champions of 1907

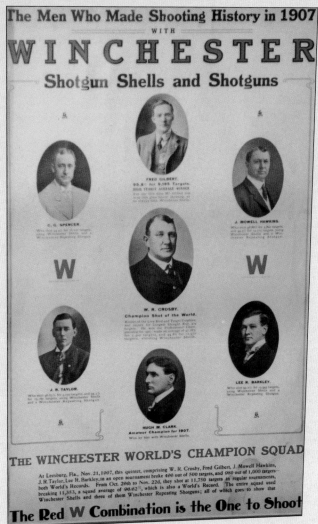

Topperwein poster. Adolph Topperwein and his wife "Plinkie" both worked for Winchester for several years conducting trickshooting exhibitions. This piece probably dates from the 1906-1908 period. The Winchester "lightning strike" logo is not used but Adolph is wearing a big white "W" on his sweater. Overall size is 21 1/2" wide x 32 1/2" high. From Tim Melcher collection. Photo by TIM.

Values: $1,500 - $1,750.

Winchester World's Champion Squad from 1907. W.R. Crosby, C.G. Spencer, Fred Gilbert, J. Mowell Hawkins, Lee R. Barkley, Hugh M. Clark, and J.R. Taylor set several shooting records in 1907 using Winchester guns and ammunition. Cardboard poster. Overall size is 14" wide x 28" high. From Dennis Mack collection. Photo by D. Mack.

Values: $1,500 - $1,750.

Black Poster - Repeating Shotguns

Black Poster - Rifles and Ammunition

Black poster - Repeating Shotguns. Uses an inventive black background and requires the viewer to imagine the "body outline" of the successful duck hunter with the big cartridge belt. Does not use the red "W" (see it's companion piece) but shows the post-1906 "lightning strike" logo typeface. Probably dates from 1906-1908. Overall size is 11 1/2" wide x 19 3/8" high. From Tom Webster collection. Photo by D. Kowalski.

Values: $1,200 - $1,500.

Black poster - Rifles and Ammunition. The "rifle" counterpart of the previous shotgun poster, again requiring the viewer to imagine the "body outline" of the shooter under the bush. Uses the new red "W" and the "lightning strike" logo typeface that were both introduced in 1906. Probably dates from 1906-1908. This poster has two holes at the top and a hanging string attached. Overall size is 11 7/8" wide x 20" high. From Dennis Mack collection. Photo by D. Mack.

Values: $1,200 - $1,500.

"Dawn of the Open Season"

"Results! Yesterday - Today - Tomorrow."

"Dawn of the Open Season" pictures two hunters and their two leashed bird dogs. Painted by N.C. Wyeth in 1910, who was also commissioned to paint the grizzly bear scene for the 1912 Winchester calendar. Overall size is 18 1/2" wide x 29 1/4" high. Metal bands top and bottom. From Tom Webster collection. Photo by D. Kowalski.

Values: $1,500 - $1,700.

Uses same painting as "Dawn of the Open Season" but this poster was not released until the fall of 1925 as part of the company's published "1926 Advertising Campaign." The 1926 ad campaign materials show a slightly different arrangement of the "Results" copy but publishes a poster size nearly identical to the one reported here. Sales campaigns require lead time so the literature for the retailers could have been sent to them before the final version of the poster was sent to the printer. Overall size is 17 1/4" wide x 25 1/8" high. Metal bands top and bottom. From Tom Webster collection. Photo by D. Kowalski.

Values: $1,700 - $2,000.

"Comrades" - National Father and Son Week

Father and Son Shooting Rabbit

"Comrades" uses the painting by George Brehm that would become the 1918 corporate calendar image. In 1917, the dates of February 11-17 span Sunday to Saturday, leading us to believe this was produced in late 1916 or early 1917 to promote that week. The poster does not carry the "Winchester" name but it's unlikely George Brehm would have been allowed to sell it to anyone else if Winchester was using it for both its 1918 ad campaign and calendar. (See next poster.) Overall size is 20 5/8" wide x 30 3/8" high. Metal bands top and bottom. From Tom Webster collection. Photo by D. Kowalski.

Values: $600 - $700.

Father and Son Shooting Rabbit. This poster is highlighted in the 1918 Advertising Campaign materials. Winchester used George Brehm's appealing painting heavily in 1917 and 1918 to reinforce overall marketing efforts for their Winchester Junior Rifle Corps concept launched in July 1917. Overall size is 17 3/4" wide x 36" high. Metal bands top and bottom. From Tom Webster collection. Photo by D. Kowalski.

Values: $1,750 - $2,000.

Boy and Black Terrier

Unit at Range - WJRC

Boy and Black Terrier. Another window poster spotlighted in the 1918 Advertising Campaign materials. Boy is holding a Model 90. He and his gun and black terrier would also be the main images promoting the Winchester Junior Rifle Corps on the first Winchester five-panel advertising display in March 1920. Only two of these posters are known to exist. Image size is 17" wide x 35" high; overall size is 17 3/4" wide x 36" high. Metal bands top and bottom. From Tom Webster collection. Photo by D. Kowalski.

Values: $5,000 - $6,000.

Unit at Range - Winchester Junior Rifle Corps. Produced in 1922. Artist believed to be George Brehm. Overall size is 17 3/4" wide x 35 3/4" high. Metal bands top and bottom. From Tom Webster collection. Photo by D. Kowalski.

Values: $4,000 - $4,500.

Get Your Boy to Join - WJRC

World Standard Target Rifles

Get Your Boy to Join the Winchester Junior Rifle Corps. Produced in 1919. Artist believed to be George Brehm. Overall size is 17 3/4" wide x 36" high. Metal bands top and bottom. From Tom Webster collection. Photo by D. Kowalski.

Values: $3,500 - $4,000.

World Standard Target and Small Game Rifles and Ammunition. Companion poster to the prior one produced in 1919. Image size is 17" wide x 35" high; overall size is 17 3/4" wide x 36" high. Metal bands top and bottom. From Tom Webster collection. Photo by D. Kowalski.

Values: $3,000 - $3,500.

Grizzly Bear on Rock above Two Hunters

Hunter on White Horse with Bear

Grizzly Bear on Rock above Two Hunters. This painting by N.C. Wyeth set the precedent for a dominant and dramatic visual element when Winchester revived wall calendars in 1912. This poster was part of the 1918 Advertising Campaign. Only two are known to exist. Image size is 17" wide x 35" high; overall size is 18" wide x 36" high with an unusual purple border (it was usually white) around the image area. Metal bands top and bottom. From Tom Webster collection. Photo by D. Kowalski.

Values: $3,800 - $4,200.

Hunter in Mountains on White Horse with Grizzly Bear behind Him. Promotes Winchester high-powered rifles and ammunition. Bottom two lines of poster read: "The Winchester Model 54, a World's Standard High Power Bolt Action Sporting Rifle Calibers 270 W.C.F. and .30 Govt. '06." Produced in 1925. (Another version without copy lines at bottom was also part of the 1926 Advertising Campaign.) Overall size is 17 1/4" wide x 36" high. Metal bands top and bottom. From Tom Webster collection. Photo by D. Kowalski.

Values: $3,800 - $4,200
         (1925 or 1926 version).

Hunter by Campfire with Bobcat

.22 Caliber Cartridges (Prototype Art)

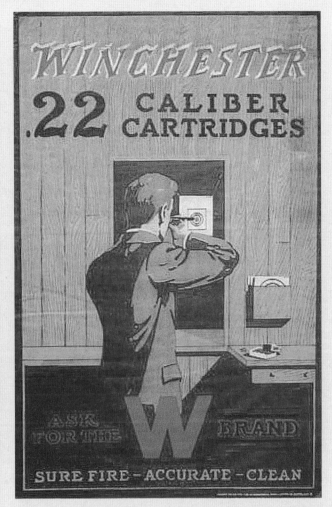

Hunter by the Campfire with Bobcat. Winchester's last poster before the Western purchase, this one was produced in 1930. Artist unknown. Live matter area is 14 5/8" wide x 25 1/8" high; overall size is 15" wide x 25 3/4" high. Metal bands top and bottom. From Tom Webster collection. Photo by D. Kowalski.

Values: $2,700 - $3,000.

.22 Caliber Cartridges - Shooter with Target. A rare piece that may be the only one in existence. It is actually printed on very thin velum paper, the kind that would then be glued to cardboard if it was to become a sign. May also have been a prototype for a small poster. Artist unknown and it was likely produced from 1906-1918. Overall size is 11 3/4" wide x 17 3/4" high. From Jennifer Hunter/Gary Gole collection. Photo by J. Hunter.

Values: $2,000 - $2,500.

World Standard Guns (Banner)

World Standard Guns and Ammunition Banner. Made of light canvas (not hemmed). In excellent condition and the only one known in this size. Overall size is 60" long x 26 1/2" high. From Tom Webster collection. Photo by D. Kowalski.

Values: $500 - $700.

Hardware, Paints (Winchester Store Banner)

Winchester Store banner promotes Hardware and Paints. Made of medium-weight canvas. Overall size is 82" long x 15" high. From Dennis Mack collection. Photo by D. Mack.

Values: $700 - $900.

Factory Loaded Shells (Banner)

Early Winchester Armory (Poster)

Winchester Armory poster shows the factory in its very early days. One of the earliest factory posters showing its original setting in the countryside. This is also the only version of this early factory scene poster that is known to exist. Winchester would occasionally use this sepia-tone brown treatment, especially on early five-panel displays. Live matter area is 34" wide x 22 1/4" high; overall size is 39 1/4" wide x 25 1/4" high. From Tom Webster collection. Photo by D. Kowalski.

Values: $1,750 - $2,200.

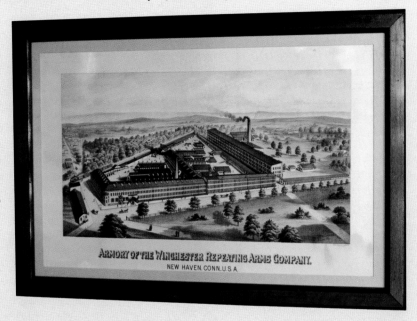

Ranger Staynless (Poster)

Small horizontal Ranger shotshell poster. Promotes the new "Staynless" primer. From the late 1920s or early 1930s. Overall size is 15 1/4" wide x 8" high. From Tim Melcher collection. Photo by TIM.

Values: $250 - $400.

Winchester banner promotes "Factory Loaded Shells" with three dramatic cutaway shells. Made of canvas (not hemmed). Very rare banner that may have been created for special event such as the Grand American Trapshoot. Overall size is 118" long x 24" high. From Tim Melcher collection. Photo by TIM.

Values: $3,500 - $4,000.

Bear Dogs (Poster)

Bear Dogs - poster version. H.R. Poore originally painted this picture of bear dogs reportedly owned by Oliver Winchester or another family member. The painting was used for the 1925 calendar, as well as an original wood-framed sign (below). To save shipping expenses and ship rolled, this posterized version was created with the frame portion photographed as part of the poster. Overall size (not including additional frame used by the collector) is 41 3/4" wide x 32 1/2" high. From Tom Webster collection. Photo by D. Kowalski.

Values: $3,500 - $3,750.

Bear Dogs (Wood-framed Sign)

Bear Dogs - Sign with original wood frame. This popular sign was shipped flat with a wood frame. Decals were used on the wood frame. Weight and transit damage led to creating the posterized version (above). This wood-framed sign is the more rare and desirable version. Image size (dogs) is 35" wide x 25 1/2" high; overall size is 41 1/2" wide x 32" high. From Tom Webster collection. Photo by D. Kowalski.

Values: $4,500 - $5,000.

Signs, Case Inserts and Die Cuts

Multi-Product Horizontal Tray (Canvas Sign)

Multiple Products on Horizontal Tray - canvas sign. Shows a broad range of Winchester products. Grommets in corners for hanging. Reportedly painted by Carl Becker and released in 1930. Only about three have been found; this one in excellent condition. Overall size is 59 1/2" long x 19" high. From Tim Melcher collection. Photo by D. Kowalski.

Values: $3,000 - $4,500.

Gallery Sign - .22 Rifle Range

.22 Live Ammunition Rifle Range - metal sign over wood frame. This one was discovered in a shooting gallery in Kansas City, Missouri. Another one from the Baltimore, Maryland area has also been found. Overall size is 72" long x 48" high. From Tom Webster collection. Photo by D. Kowalski.

Values:
$3,250 - $3,500.

Choice of Champs
(Mirror Sign)

Choice of Champs - framed mirror sign. Frame appears to be original. Perhaps only a few were ever made for key offices; only two have ever been found. Mother of pearl inlaid inside the "W." The "choice of champs" slogan was reportedly used briefly about 1910. Mirror size is 14 1/2" wide x 10 1/4" high; overall size is 18 1/2" wide x 14" high. From Tim Melcher collection. Photo by TIM.

Values: $1,750 - $2,000.

Shooting Gallery -
Metal Flange Signs

Shooting Gallery - heavy metal flange sign. Each has identical graphics and copy on both sides. Vertical sign shows the 2-inch-wide metal flange (15 1/2" long) used to mount to wall. Both also show evidence of having been damaged by someone with more bullets than brains. Overall size: horizontal version is 25 3/4" long x 19 1/4" high; vertical one is 17 3/4" wide and 27 1/2" high. Both from Tim Melcher collection. Photos by D. Kowalski.

Values: $2,500 - $2,750 (either version).

Cartridges and Guns
"Green Door" (Tin Signs)

Cartridges and Guns "Green Door" - tin sign over wood frame. Painting by Alexander Pope (1849-1924) done in 1912. English versions are much more common than Spanish ones. Each is 30" wide x 36" high. Both from Tom Webster collection. Photos by D. Kowalski.

Values: $2,000 - $3,200 (either version).

Fishing Tackle (Cardboard)

Fishing Tackle - cardboard sign with easel back. Painting of two fishermen and the jumping bass is also one of the six scenes from the 1930 calendar. Overall size is 20 1/4" wide x 15" high. From Dan Snowden collection. Photo by D. Snowden.

Values: $1,500 - $1,750.

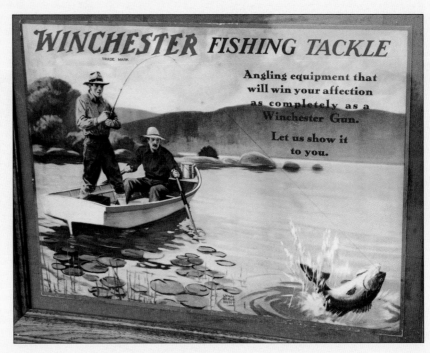

Junior Trap Shooting Outfit
(Counter Sign)

Junior Trap Shooting was a "whole new field of sport" promoted to young people beginning in 1920. Winchester took their basic Junior Rifle Corps Kit and made a shotgun version with small thrower, small clay targets and choice of single shot shotguns. Cardboard counter sign is rare and measures 16 3/4" wide x 8" high. From Tom Webster collection. Photo by D. Kowalski.

Values: $1,500 - $2,000.

Trap Shooting, Utility Oil
(Counter Signs)

"Trap Shooting" promotes the Junior Trap Shooting Kit launched in 1920. "General Utility Oil" was part of fairly significant ongoing efforts to promote lubricants. Both signs are part of series of cardboard counter signs with easel backs done in 1920. Both are 8 1/2" wide x 10 1/2" high. From Tim Melcher collection. Photo by TIM.

**Values: $250 - $400 (Utility Oil);
$350 - $500 (Junior Trap Shooting).**

Gallery Shooters - .22 Cartridges (Hanging Sign)

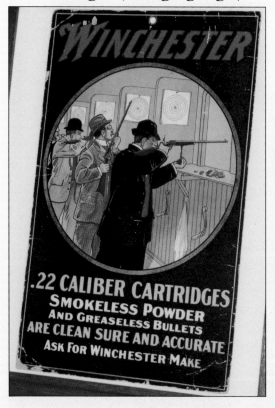

Four Shooters at the Shooting Gallery, .22 Caliber cartridges - an early cardboard hanging sign. The "Winchester" logo typeface is identical to that used on the 1904 "Three Mallard Ducks Flying" poster. Note the "devil's tail" on the far right upstroke of the "W." Overall size is 8 1/2" wide x 14" high. From Don Alters collection. Photo by D. Alters.

Values: $2,000 - $2,250.

Leader (Hanging Tin Sign)

Leader - hanging embossed tin sign. Shows a "Winchester" logo style from pre-1906. Size is 13 1/2" wide x 9 3/4" high. From Curt Bowman collection. Photos by C. Bowman.

Values: $1,000- $1,500.

Winchester Ammunition (Hanging Signs)

Winchester Ammunition - cardboard hanging sign. May be one of the first hanging signs. Uses a "Winchester" logo typeface typical of the 1890s. The cartridge headstamp reads: "WRACO. 45-90 W.C.F." - a shell Winchester first produced in 1886. Size is 14 3/4" wide x 8 7/8" high. From Tim Melcher collection. Photo by TIM.

Values: $1,000 - $1,500.

Nublack, New Rival
(Hanging Signs)

Nublack, New Rival - hanging signs. Nublack and New Rival signs both cardboard. Probably from late teens or early 1920s. Size of each is 16 3/4" wide x 10 1/8" high. From Curt Bowman collection. Photos by C. Bowman.

Values: $2,500 - $3,000 (Nublack);
$2,300 - $2,800 (New Rival).

"Case Insert" Hanging Signs ...
Do You Shoot? (left); The Hunters'
Choice (above); A Drummer (right);
The Kind You Need (far right)

These four are called "case inserts" because these cardboard hanging signs were shipped to retailers in the top of a case of 12 gauge shells, then displayed in the store. The three with vertical formats were probably produced first because they all have the same pre-1906 logo typeface. They measure 8 1/8" wide x 12 1/8" high. "The Hunters' Choice" is rarest. "Do You Shoot?" done after 1906 because it has "lightning strike" logo. It's also the only one showing a firearm (Model 97) or a horizontal format, and is slightly smaller - 12" wide x 8" high. All from Tom Webster collection. Photos by D. Kowalski.

Values: $1,200 - $1,800; add 10 percent for
"The Hunters' Choice."

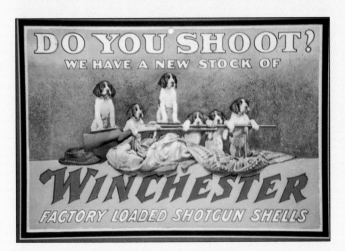

Grouse Flying
(Large "Case Insert")

Flying Grouse with Repeater Shell Box - large "case insert" hanging cardboard sign. Produced later than the other four on these two pages (probably late teens or early 1920s). Slightly larger, it would have fit in a case of 10 gauge shells. Only two have ever been found. Size is 13 5/8" wide x 9 1/4" high. From Tom Webster collection. Photo by D. Kowalski.

Values: $2,000 - $2,500.

The Kind You Need! ... Winchester Factory Loaded Shotgun Shells You Can Get Them Here.

Winchester Factory Loaded Shotgun Shells — A Drummer — The Kind For Hunting — We Have A Full Stock

Winchester Rarities • 67

The Government Experts
(Hanging Sign)

The Government Experts - cardboard hanging sign. May be from the 1930s, perhaps even early 1940s. Image size is 16 1/2" wide x 11 1/2" high; overall size is 17 3/8" wide x 12 3/8" high. From Tom Webster collection. Photo by D. Kowalski.

Values: $250 - $400.

Red W Shot Gun Shells
(Die-Cut Sign)

Ask For - Red W Shot Gun Shells Sold Here. Probably one of Winchester's earliest "cut-out" (as they called them) or "die-cut" cardboard hanging signs. Shows the red "W" introduced in 1906 but still retains a "Winchester" logo used prior to the "lightning strike" logo of 1906. Size is 6 1/2" wide x 9 3/4" high. From Tom Webster collection. Photo by D. Kowalski.

Values: $400 - $600.

Double New Rival Shell
(Die-Cut Sign)

Double New Rival Shell with Cutaway on left - die-cut sign. We believe it was used as a sign. However, there is advertising copy on the back. We doubt it was created as a "booklet" giveaway; the small piece of connecting cardboard between the two shells would not have lasted long as a folded "hinge." We include it at this point because it's an early die-cut with a pre-1906 "Winchester" logo. Size is 12 1/4" long x 2" high. From Tom Webster collection. Photo by D. Kowalski.

Values: $450 - $600.

Rifles, Shotguns - Pyramid Hanging Sign

Rifles, Shotguns - pyramid hanging sign. Each triangular cardboard panel could be folded in, then secured with the red string to make the hanging "pyramid." The bottom has line that reads: "Patented Feb. 9th 1909." This is the only one for rifles and shotguns ever found. Each panel is 8" wide at base x 15" high. From Tom Webster collection. Photo by D. Kowalski.

Values:
$7,000 - $8,500.

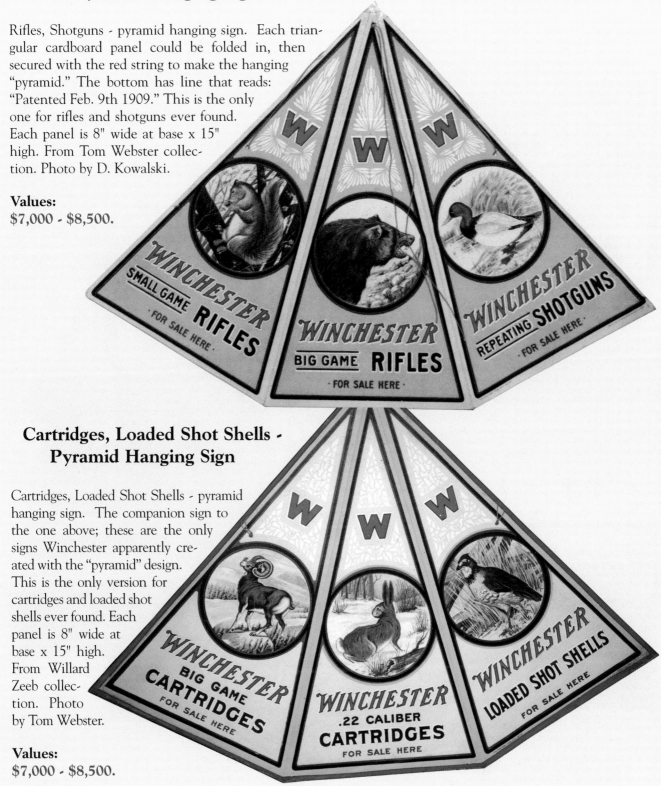

Cartridges, Loaded Shot Shells - Pyramid Hanging Sign

Cartridges, Loaded Shot Shells - pyramid hanging sign. The companion sign to the one above; these are the only signs Winchester apparently created with the "pyramid" design. This is the only version for cartridges and loaded shot shells ever found. Each panel is 8" wide at base x 15" high. From Willard Zeeb collection. Photo by Tom Webster.

Values:
$7,000 - $8,500.

Big Buck, Orange Boxes
(Die-Cut Sign)

Big Buck with Orange Cartridge Boxes - die-cut cardboard hanging sign. This is one of the rarest die-cut signs and promotes Big Game Cartridges. It's the only one ever found to date. These orange label boxes shown were produced from 1906-1910. Size is 15" wide x 15 3/8" high. From Curt Bowman collection. Photo by C. Bowman.

Values: $3,700 - $4,000.

Kneeling Hunter and Burro
(Die-Cut Sign)

Kneeling Hunter and Burro - die-cut cardboard hanging sign. This sign shows a .30 caliber W.C.F. cartridge with "W.R.A. Co." headstamp. Produced after 1906. Size is 7 1/4" wide x 11 7/8" high. From Curt Bowman collection. Photo by C. Bowman.

Values: $2,500 - $2,800

Red W Cleaning Preparations
(Die-Cut Sign)

Red W Cleaning Preparations - die-cut cardboard hanging sign. Promotes gun cleaning products. Produced about 1910. Size is 8" wide x 15" high. From Tim Melcher collection. Photo by TIM.

Values: $700 - $900.

Pistol and Holster Belt
(Die-Cut Sign)

Pistol and Holster Belt - die-cut cardboard hanging sign. Another extremely rare die-cut sign, as this is the only example ever found. Very few signs promoted pistol cartridges and no others are known that picture a holster. Probably a creation from the 1906-1910 era. Size is 11 1/2" wide x 11" high. From Tom Turigliatti collection. Photo by T. Turigliatti.

Values: $3,500 - $3,750.

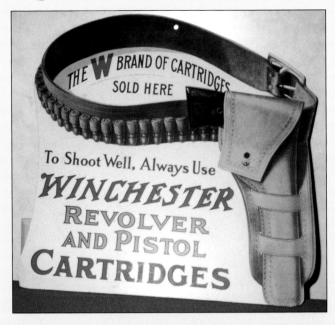

Dog, Two Quail, 10 Shells
(Die-Cut Sign)

Dog, Two Quail, 10 shells - die-cut cardboard hanging sign. This sign promotes Leader, Repeater and Nublack shotgun shells. Probably from the 1906-1910 era (Nublack loaded shells introduced in 1905). Size is 7 1/8" wide x 12" high. From Tom Webster collection. Photo by D. Kowalski.

Values: $1,750 - $2,000.

Flying Gamebirds
(Three Round Die-Cut Signs)

Flying woodcock ("Repeater"), quail ("New Rival") and grouse ("Nublack") - round die-cut cardboard hanging signs. A fourth sign from this group shows four flying Canada geese ("Leader"). These were probably created in 1906-1910 era. Each shell name has quote marks around it, unusual for Winchester signs, unless its marketing department wanted to introduce a new brand name (as they were with Nublack loaded shells which came out in 1905). Sizes are 9 3/4" wide x 10" high. From Curt Bowman collection. Photo by C. Bowman.

Values: $1,700 - $2,000 (any version).

Boy on Fence Holding Rabbit
(Die-Cut Sign)

Boy on Fence Holding Rabbit - die-cut cardboard hanging sign. This extremely rare die-cut sign is the only example ever found. And very few advertising pieces ever showed a Model 90. Probably produced from 1906-1920. Size is 9" wide x 14" high. From Willard Zeeb collection. Photo by T. Webster.

Values: $3,700 - $4,000.

Hunter Hooked
on Wire Fence
(Die-Cut Sign)

Hunter Hooked on Barbed Wire Fence - die-cut cardboard hanging sign. This sign shows Repeater shotshell box from the early 1920s. About four or five of these signs have been found. Size is 7 1/2" wide x 12" high. From Don Alters collection. Photo by D. Alters.

Values: $2,700 - $3,000.

Woodcock on Fence Rail
(Die-Cut Sign)

Woodcock on Wooden Fence Rail - die-cut cardboard hanging sign. This sign shows Leader, Repeater, Nublack, and New Rival shotshell boxes from the early 1920s. Only a few of these signs have ever been found. Size is 8 1/4" wide x 12 1/2" high. From Curt Bowman collection. Photo by C. Bowman.

Values: $3,200 - $3,500.

Grouse, Leader Shells and Box (Die-Cut Sign)

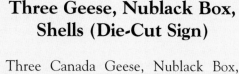

Standing Grouse, Two Leader Shells, Leader Box - die-cut cardboard hanging sign. Only a few examples have been found. Produced in the early 1920s. Size is 7 3/8" wide x 12" high. From Tom Webster collection. Photo by D. Kowalski.

Values: $3,200 - $3,500.

Three Geese, Nublack Box, Shells (Die-Cut Sign)

Three Canada Geese, Nublack Box, Four Shells - die-cut cardboard hanging sign. Also produced in the early 1920s. About five have been found. Size is 7" wide x 11 7/8" high. From Curt Bowman collection. Photo by C. Bowman.

Values: $3,200 - $3,500.

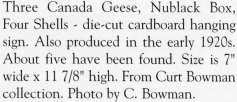

Leader Box, Nublack Box (Die-Cut Signs)

Leader Box (above), Nublack Box (right) - die-cut cardboard hanging signs. These are the same boxes on the larger die-cuts positioned above. Repeater Box is also part of the group (not pictured; see box example on bottom of "Hooked Hunter" sign on facing page). Produced early 1920s. Each is 8 3/8" wide x 8 3/8" high. From Curt Bowman collection. Photos by C. Bowman.

Values: $500 - $600 (Leader version); $700 - $900 (Nublack or Repeater versions).

Boy, Rock Wall
(3-D Die-Cut Counter Sign)

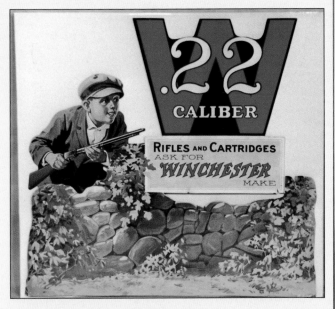

Boy with Model '06, Rock Wall - 3-D die-cut cardboard counter sign. This sign used two pieces set up for a 3-D effect. Probably produced in the 1906-1915 era. Size is 13 5/8" wide x 12 5/8" high. From Tom Webster collection. Photo by D. Kowalski.

Values: $3,000 - $3,500.

Leaping Whitetail Buck,
Big Horn Ram and Ewe
(3-D Die-Cut Counter Signs)

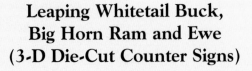

Leaping Whitetail Buck (above right) and Leaping Big Horn Ram and Ewe (right) - 3-D die-cut cardboard counter signs. This companion set was designed to promote rifles and cartridges. Each is two pieces (with tab-and-slot design) that could be set up for 3-D effect. Probably produced in the 1906-1915 era. Both painted by Lynn Bogue Hunt and only one example of each has ever been found. Size of each is 11 5/8" wide x 15" high. From Tom Webster collection. Photos by D. Kowalski.

Values: $3,700 - $4,000 (either version).

Black Guide with White Hunter
(Die-Cut Counter Sign)

Black Guide with White Hunter - die-cut cardboard counter sign. This is the only example of this sign known to exist. Produced after 1906. Winchester did not use many black people in its advertising. The other notable example is the controversial "Shoot Them and Avoid Trouble" poster issued in 1908. Size is 8 1/4" wide x 9 3/4" high. From Don Alters collection. Photo by D. Alters.

Values: $2,750 - $3,000.

Leaping White Ram
(3-D Die-Cut Counter Sign)

Leaping White Ram - 3-D die-cut cardboard counter sign. This sign uses the same "Ask for Winchester Make" copy as "Boy and Rock Wall" sign on facing page. Appear to be companion signs: this one for larger revolver and pistol cartridges; the other for .22 rifles and shells. Size is 10 1/4" wide x 14 3/4" high. From Curt Bowman collection. Photo by C. Bowman.

Values: $3,000 - $3,500.

Breech Loading Cannon
(Die-Cut Counter Sign)

Breech Loading Cannon - die-cut cardboard counter sign. Winchester introduced the "Salute Cannon" in 1903. This sign, the only one known to exist, probably dates from 1906-1912 era. In 1912, Winchester started using the image of two crossed "Blue Rival" shells (with one corrugation around shell head) on shotshell boxes for that brand. Note distinctive "Ask for Winchester Make" copy (see above); such phrases tend to get used for a while, then abandoned for some new creative slogan. Size is 17" wide x 15" high. From Willard Zeeb collection. Photo by T. Webster.

Values: $3,750 - $4,000.

Champion Shooters
(Die-Cut Counter Signs)

Fred Gilbert, W.R. Crosby, J.A.R. Elliott - die-cut cardboard counter signs (left, top to bottom). All these signs promote Leader shotshells and all are very rare. These three shooters were among the noted match shooters Winchester sponsored in the early 1900s. Probably created in the 1906-1910 time period. Sizes: Crosby - 15" wide x 16 1/8" high; Elliott - 15 1/4" high x 16 1/8" high; Gilbert - 15" wide x 15 7/8" high. From Curt Bowman collection. Photos by C. Bowman.

Values: $4,000 - $4,300.

C.G. Spencer - 96.77%
(Die-Cut Counter Sign)

C.G. Spencer, The Man, The Gun and The Shells (96.77%) - die-cut cardboard counter sign. This sign promotes Repeater and Leader shells and may have been produced ten years or more after the other three on this page. Shell boxes shown are from late teens or early 1920s. A very rare sign. Size is 10" wide x 22" high. From Tom Webster collection. Photo by D. Kowalski.

Values: $4,000 - $4,300.

Quail, Repeater Box, Two Shells
(Die-Cut Counter Sign)

Quail, Repeater Box, Leader and Repeater Shells - die-cut cardboard counter sign. The shell box has extended trademark line, "Trade Mark Reg. U.S. Pat. Off. And Throughout the World" used from 1912-1917. Size is 8" wide x 11 1/8" high. From Tom Webster collection. Photo by D. Kowalski.

Values: $2,500 - $2,800.

Antelope Heads
(Die-Cut Counter Signs)

Pronghorn Antelope (American) and European/ African Antelope (French version) - die-cut cardboard counter signs. Probably produced between 1906-1920. The American version is 9 1/4" wide x 12" high; the French is 8 1/4" wide x 12 1/8" high. From Tom Webster collection. Photos by D. Kowalski.

Values: $1,000 - $1,500 (American);
$500 - $700 (French).

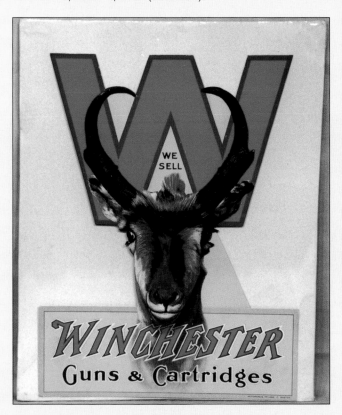

Big Shotshells, Gamebirds (Die-Cut Counter Signs)

Geese & Blue New Rival Shell; Woodcock & Yellow Repeater Shell; Quail & Yellow Nublack Shell; and Grouse & Orange Leader Shell - die-cut cardboard counter signs. Produced for the 1918 advertising campaign, each measures 12 3/4" wide x 10 7/8" high. The Grouse with Leader Shell from Tom Webster collection; photo by D. Kowalski. Others from Curt Bowman collection; photos by C. Bowman.

Values: $1,800 - $2,200 (any version).

Jacksnipe to Wild Turkey
(Die-Cut Counter Sign)

From Jacksnipe to Wild Turkey - die-cut cardboard counter sign. A rare piece; only two are currently known. This sign promoted Leader and Repeater shotshells for the 1926 advertising campaign. Painted by Lynn Bogue Hunt. Size is 10" wide x 15" high. From Tom Webster collection. Photo by D. Kowalski.

Values: $3,000 - $3,400.

Grizzly to Squirrel
(Die-Cut Counter Sign)

From the Grizzly to the Squirrel - die-cut cardboard counter sign. A companion piece to "Wild Turkey" (right); this one promotes metallic ammunition. Also produced for the 1926 advertising campaign. Size is 13" wide x 21 3/4" high. From Curt Bowman collection. Photo by C. Bowman.

Values: $1,250 - $1,500.

Ranger Box, Shell
(Die-Cut Counter Sign)

Ranger, New Smokeless Shotshell - die-cut cardboard counter sign. Ranger shotshells were first advertised in July 1924. This was a very early (perhaps the first) Ranger die-cut created for the 1926 advertising campaign. Painted by Lynn Bogue Hunt, it measures 10 1/8" wide x 15" high. From Tom Webster collection. Photo by D. Kowalski.

Values: $1,750 - $2,000.

In The Bag
(Die-Cut Counter Sign)

In The Bag - die-cut cardboard counter sign. Pictured in a full-page ad in the September 1928 issue of Outdoor Life. This sign was painted by Lynn Bogue Hunt. Size is 18 3/4" wide x 26 1/2" high. From Tom Webster collection. Photo by D. Kowalski.

Values: $2,250 - $2,500.

New Model 60
(Die-Cut
Counter Sign)

New Model 60 Single Shot .22 - die-cut cardboard counter sign. The Model 60 was introduced in 1931, then discontinued in 1933. Kopperklad bullets were introduced in 1929. Size is 15" wide x 28 3/8" high. From Dennis Mack collection. Photo by D. Mack.

Values: $1,750 - $2,000.

Model 60
(Die-Cut Brochure)

The Greatest Value Ever Offered in a Single Shot .22 - die-cut tri-fold brochure. Winchester tried a die-cutting experiment with this brochure touting New Model 60. Far left is folded piece measuring 3 1/8" wide x 6 1/8" high. The open brochure (below), shows a bold price announcement and the butt of the rifle sticking out of the side of the flap. This price flap then flipped up to give the customer a full page of advertising copy about the Model 60. The half-open brochure is 9 1/4" wide x 6 1/8" high. From Tom Webster collection. Photo by D. Kowalski.

Values: $150 - $250.

Staynless Series
(Die-Cut Counter Signs)

Guns and Shells; Sporting Rifles and Ammunition; Guns and Ammunition - die-cut counter signs. This is a set of three signs promoting "Staynless, Lacquered" and "Kopperklad" ammo done after 1929; we see both "Laquered" shotshells and "Kopperklad" .22 shells - both 1929 introductions. The "Guns and Shells" version (right) also shows the unique 10-shell box of Leader shotshells. This one and the "Whitetail" version (below right) were both painted by Lynn Bogue Hunt. Sizes: "Guns and Shells" - 19 1/2" wide x 28 3/4" high; "Sporting Rifles and Ammunition" - 19" wide x 27 7/8" wide. Both from Tom Webster collection. Photos by D. Kowalski.

Values: $1,200 - $1,500.

The "Guns and Ammunition" version (below) is one of the finest ever found without the typical damage to the pheasant's tail. Size is 21 1/2" wide x 28" high. From Dan Snowden collection. Photo by D. Snowden.

Values: $1,750 - $2,000.

Super Speed .22s
(Die-Cut Counter Signs)

Airplane and Speeding Bullet (left), Stack of Boards with Bullet Hole (lower left) - die-cut counter signs. Both promote Super Speed .22s. The red and white "Super W Speed" box on the top sign dates this die-cut at 1932, when this box color/ design was launched. The bottom sign shows the next Super Speed box, the Yellow/Blue/Red box, which various writers have dated from 1936 to 1938. This sign has a "Copyrighted 1935" notation at the bottom, now clearly establishing that the Yellow/Blue/Red box was being marketed in 1935. Sizes: top - 22 1/4" wide x 27 1/2" high; bottom - 19 5/8" wide x 26 3/8" wide. Both from Tom Webster collection. Photos by D. Kowalski.

Values: $500 - $700 (either version).

Rearing Grizzly and Flying Mallards
(Point-of-Purchase Signs)

"Rearing Grizzly" - Rifles (left above), "Flying Mallards - Shotguns (right) - end pieces of POP display. Produced after 1927, when Winchester introduced the "Staynless" loadings in the pictured "Blue/White" boxes. Left sign pictures a box of .30 (.30-30) Soft Points. Right sign shows Repeater and Repeater Speed Loads, Leader and Ranger shells in 10 and 12 gauge. Sizes: left - 15 1/2" wide x 38" high; right - 14 7/8" wide x 37 1/2" wide. Both from Tom Webster collection. Photos by D. Kowalski.

Values: $1,750 - $2,000 (either version).

Point-of-Purchase Displays

1914 Window Display   **(Poster and Die-Cut Signs)**

Guns and Cartridges - 1914 Window Display - poster and two die-cuts (above). Perhaps the first of the large Point-of-Purchase displays. The center poster, painted by Philip R. Goodwin, is on light paper and measures 60" wide x 40 1/8" high; it was folded twice in original box. Side pieces are heavy cardboard with easel backs. The left one is Robert Robinson's painting of bearded hunter from 1913 calendar; it is 20" wide x 28 1/2" high. Right die-cut is Goodwin's man on snowshoes from his 1906 Winchester poster; it is 20" wide x 28" high. Tom Webster purchased set (one of two complete sets known) in a sealed box identified as a "1914 Window Display." From Tom Webster collection. Photo by D. Kowalski.

Values: $4,750 - $5,000.

Hunter and Guide   **(POP Display)**

Hunter and Guide - POP display. Perhaps the earliest all-cardboard POP display. Has same emblem as above display; these are the only two displays we've seen where Winchester used this emblem; it reads: "Rice Leaders of the World Association - Be Guided by this Foundation"; includes words "Strength, Honor, Quality, Service."* Winchester tended to use certain graphic elements for a period of time, then switched to something new. Size of the center section is 30" wide x 39 5/8" high. Each wing measures 36" wide x 19" high. (Far left panel reads "Self-Loading Shotguns" at bottom.) From Tom Webster collection. Photo by D. Kowalski.

Values: $4,250 - $4,500.

* Winchester sponsored a contest beginning in 1914 and ending May 15, 1915, seeking more Association members. The 1914 Window Display instruction sheet described the contest and named about 25 other members including Elgin National Watch Co., Remington Typewriter Co., National Veneer Products and American Optical Co. The emblem also appears on the 1916 Winchester 50th Anniversary invitation.

Two Hunters, Two Dogs Having Lunch
(POP Display)

Two Hunters, Two Dogs Having Lunch - POP display. Another very early one showing Model 12 shotguns. Measures 63" wide x 42 1/4" high. From Curt Bowman collection. Photo by C. Bowman.

Values: $4,250 - $4,500.

Two Hunters at Campsite (POP Display)

Two Hunters at Campsite - POP display. Shows box of Repeater shotshells from late teens or early 1920s. Size is 40 1/4" wide x 30 1/8" high. From Tim Melcher collection. Photo by TIM.

Values: $3,750 - $4,000.

Three Boys, Two Hunters (POP Display)

Three Boys, Two Hunters - POP display. Created for the 1918 Advertising Campaign. Painted by Hy S. Watson in 1917. Size is 59 1/2" wide x 40" high. From Tim Melcher collection. Photo by D. Kowalski.

Values: $4,000 - $4,250.

Repeater, Leader Box Pyramid (POP Display)

Repeater and Leader Box Pyramid - POP display. Shows three Repeater and six Leader shotshell boxes with labels from late teens or early 1920s. The blue box in middle is only meant to be a description panel, not a photo of an actual retail box. Size is 18" wide x 18" high (also 9 1/2" deep since this sets up in "stair-step" fashion. From Tim Melcher collection. Photo by TIM.

Values: $3,750 - $4,000.

Father and Son in Duck Boat (POP Display)

Father and Son in Duck Boat - POP display. Scene from 1920 calendar used to create a large easel-back display. The only one ever found to date. Size is 33 3/4" wide x 25 1/4" high. From Tom Webster collection. Photo by D. Kowalski.

Values: $2,750 - $3,000.

Heavy Gun Oil
(POP Display)

Heavy Gun Oil - POP counter display. Would have held six bottles in 1 oz. size. Probably dates from 1906-1910 since it has the "lightning strike" logo. Box is 11 1/2" long x 5" wide; flap in upright position is 7" from top to counter. From Tim Melcher collection. Photo by TIM.

Values: $500 - $750 (display only).

Pocketknife Display Box
(POP Display)

Pocketknife Display Box. Twelve pocketknives with assorted fancy celluloid handles came in this self-contained display box for the counter. The display box was pulled out of the cardboard covering sleeve and the top display flap turned up. Box size is 10 1/2" long x 3 7/8" wide; display flap turned up is 4" from top to the counter. From Dennis Mack collection. Photo by D. Mack.

**Values: $3,750 - $4,000
(with original 12 knives).**

Roller Skate Counter Display
(POP Display)

Roller Skate Counter Display. Probably dates from 1920s, although Winchester would continue to produce roller skates after the 1931 Western takeover. Size is 15" wide x 23 1/2" high. From Dennis Mack collection. Photo by D. Mack.

Values: $500 - $750.

Guns and Ammunition
(POP Display)

Guns and Ammunition - POP display. Has six folds and seven panels to create 3-D effect when set up. The only example of this one ever found. Copyright is 1923. Painted by G. Ryder, who also painted 1924 calendar scene. Shotshells shown are Repeater 12 gauge. Cartridges are .30 Winchester Model 94 Soft Point (left) and .405 caliber, 300 grain (right). Size is 82 1/4" wide x 40 1/4" high. From Tom Webster collection. Photo by D. Kowalski.

Values: $4,250 - $4,500.

The Perfect Pattern Shell
(POP Display)

The Perfect Pattern Shell - POP display. The absence of a Ranger box dates this as pre-1924. Size is 50 1/4" wide x 35" high. From Tom Webster collection. Photo by D. Kowalski.

Values: $2,750 - $3,000.

We Know ... Are Good
("Cartoon" POP Display)

We Know ... Are Good - POP display. Winchester produced very few POP displays in "cartoon" format. Each piece has its own easel back. Ranger box dates this after 1924. As an aside, whenever Winchester produced a display, they sent a set-up sheet showing all the pieces to the retailer or put line-art of the display on the back of the main panel. Some collectors would buy only a side panel such as we see here and claim it was an independent display. Full display is 69 1/2" wide x 42 1/2" high. From Tom Webster collection. Photo by D. Kowalski.

Values: $3,500 - $3,750.

Fishing Tackle
(POP Display)

Fishing tackle - POP display. Winchester produced very few POP displays for fishing tackle. Probably created in the 1923-1929 era. This is the only one like this ever found. Tabs on lower panel fit into slots to create three-faced, curved back as a stand. Overall size is 42" wide x 30" high; tackle and lures panel is 29 1/2" wide x 8" high. From Tom Webster collection. Photo by D. Kowalski.

Values: $4,750 - $5,000.

Two Deer Hunters in Canoe (POP Display)

Two Deer Hunters in Canoe - POP display. Show first Ranger boxes on lower left (introduced 1924) and "Precision" .22 boxes with red band on lower right (1923), making this a piece likely done in 1924, especially since Winchester is touting shooting performances from 1922 and 1923. NOT painted by Philip R. Goodwin, as some have speculated. Size is 56" wide x 38" high. From Tom Webster collection. Photo by D. Kowalski.

Values: $1,750 - $2,000.

Cowboy on White Horse with Grizzly (POP Display)

Cowboy on White Horse with Grizzly Bear - POP display. The painting from the center panel was first introduced in 1925. Also has first Ranger boxes. This is the only one of these displays ever found that we're aware of. Size is 80 3/4" wide x 36 1/8" high. From Tom Webster collection. Photo by D. Kowalski.

Values: $4,000 - $4,250.

Guns and Shells - Results! (POP Display)

Guns and Shells - Results! - POP display. Uses the phrase "Results! Yesterday, today, tomorrow" found on two pieces from 1926 Advertising Campaign. This display was probably created as additional material after that campaign was announced. Has 3-D panel at middle front. Overall size is 54 1/2" wide x 31" high. From Curt Bowman collection. Photo by C. Bowman.

Values: $3,750 - $4,000.

Quality Products - Mountain Man (POP Display)

Quality Products - Mountain Man (with book) - POP display. The painting from the 1930 calendar became the centerpiece of this display. In addition, the individual scenes from the calendar pages were added as a "book" with two additional large folded, double pages held with a center staple. Main display is 30 1/4" wide x 40" high. From Tom Webster collection. Photo by D. Kowalski.

Values: $1,750 - $2,000 (with all book pages).

Great Guns and Ammunition (POP Display)

Great Guns and Ammunition - POP display. Shows Models 12 and 21 on left; 54 and 55 on right. Copyrighted in 1932. Overall size is 37 7/8" wide x 31 1/4" high. From Tom Webster collection. Photo by D. Kowalski.

Values: $1,800 - $2,200.

Guns and Ammunition, Hunters with Beagle (POP Display)

Guns and Ammunition - Hunters with Beagle - POP display. Shows Models 42, 21 and 12 on left; 54, 64 and 63 on right. Copyrighted in 1932. Painted by Arthur D. Fuller. Size is 42 1/4" wide x 32" high. From Tim Melcher collection. Photo by TIM.

Values: $1,750 - $2,000.

A Good Harvest (POP Display)

A Good Harvest Comes from Good Planting - POP display. Continues the game conservation, winter feeding and game harvest themes also used in the companion display below. Copyrighted in 1934. Also painted by Philip R. Goodwin. Size is 42 1/4" wide (as shown) x 41 3/4" high. From Curt Bowman collection. Photo by C. Bowman.

Values: $2,750 - $3,000.

Planting Game Feed Pays (POP Display)

Planting Game Feed Pays - POP display. Such boxes as Win. .270 Staynless Non-Mercuric and .32 Win. Special Staynless Non-Mercuric put this display at 1932 (when "Non-Mercuric" was first added to cartridge boxes for a time) to perhaps 1935. Painted by Philip R. Goodwin, who rarely painted upland game scenes. Size is 33 1/2" wide (as shown but longer extended) x 37 1/8" high. From Tom Webster collection. Photo by D. Kowalski.

Values: $2,750 - $3,000.

Five–Panel Window Displays

Perhaps no other major category of Winchester collectibles has been ignored for as long as the Five-Panel Window Displays. Their large size was probably the chief reason. Each of the five panels in a set is 40 inches high and 19 inches wide, requiring a display area more than 8 feet long.

The first five-panel set went out to Winchester retailers for the seven-day period of March 4-10, 1920. For display purposes, Winchester's "week" started on Thursday and ended on Wednesday. These first sets only had scenes on one side, a practice that would continue through September, 1920. Then both sides were printed with distinct scenes and themes targeted at specific "weeks." Since these target weeks were sometimes two or three months apart, retailers had their own storage problems with them.

We present the full sets available to us in what we believe is the correct chronological order, thanks to the diligent research of Thomas I. "Tim" Melcher. He spent hundreds of hours immersed in original Winchester documents to both identify these five-panel sets and then determine their order of release. We are immensely indebted to him for sharing this research and helping us translate it for you. We arranged the sets by their date of first use, whether they were to be used once or several times.

Our best guess is that five-panel sets were produced through 1928. (As we moved toward the end of this time period, precise documentation became more difficult to obtain but we forged ahead and dated the sets as best we could.)

We believe the 29 one-sided sets and 47 two-sided sets in this volume are about 80 percent of the total sets produced. We have access to several more incomplete sets but decided to omit them for space reasons or because, in some cases, we were not sure what the entire set even looked like.

This is the most complete presentation of five-panel sets ever attempted. For that we owe another huge debt of gratitude to Oren R. White. His heroic efforts to make sure we had great photographs of his outstanding collection have enriched this book beyond measure. Tim Melcher's collection provided another huge source of key sets, supported by his collection of the small counter stands produced to match many (perhaps all) of the five-panel scenes created the first year.

Finally, we apologize for omitting Winchester's "official" set names and code numbers. Our goal was not to get bogged down in volumes of historical minutiae. Our goal was to give you the biggest-ever visual smorgasbord of this unique category.

Winchester Junior Rifle Corps
(March 4-10, 1920)

The first set. It is the only one known. From Tom Webster collection. Photo by D. Kowalski.

Values: $4,500 - $5,000.

Automobile Tools
(March 11-17, 1920)

From Oren R. White collection.

Values: $1,750 - $2,000.

All Kinds of Paints
(March 25-31, 1920)

From Oren R. White collection.

Values: $750 - $1,000.

High Trapshooting Scores
(April 1-7, 1920)

From Oren R. White collection.

Values: $2,750 - $3,000.

Housekeeping Utensils
(April 8-14, 1920)

From Oren R. White collection.

Values: $750 - $1,000.

Kitchen Cutlery
(April 15-21, 1920)

From Oren R. White collection.

Values: $750 - $1,000.

Beautify Your Home
(April 22-28, 1920)

From Oren R. White collection.

Values: $750 - $1,000.

Flashlights, Batteries
(April 29 - May 5, 1920)

From Oren R. White collection.

Values: $750 - $1,000.

Motoring, Picnic Scene
(May 6-12, 1920)

From Oren R. White collection.

Values: $750 - $1,000.

Roller Skates
(May 13-19, 1920)

Also shows label from original factory shipper. From Oren R. White collection.

Values: $750 - $1,000.

Bridal Gifts
(May 20-26, 1920)

From Oren R. White collection.

Values: $750 - $1,000.

Junior Trap Shooting Outfit
(May 27 - June 2, 1920)

From Tim Melcher collection. Photo by TIM.

Values: $3,500 - $3,750.

Good Fishing
(June 3-9, 1920)

From Oren R. White collection.

Values: $2,750 - $3,000.

Boy Scout Building Dock
(June 10-16, 1920)

From Oren R. White collection.

Values: $1,250 - $1,500.

Refrigerator, Ice Cream Freezer
(June 17-23, 1920)

From Oren R. White collection.

Values: $750 - $1,000.

Junior Trap Shooting Outfit, Woman on Wall
(June 24-30, 1920)

The young boy is shooting a .22 but the Junior Trap Shooting Outfit is pictured. From Oren R. White collection.

Values: $3,500 - $4,000.

Picnic Scene by Lake
(July 1-7, 1920)

From Oren R. White collection.

Values: $750 - $1,000.

Flashlights, Car Repair
(July 8-14, 1920)

From Oren R. White collection. Small counter sign measures 8 1/2" wide x 10 1/2" high; from Tim Melcher collection. Photo by TIM.

Values: $1,000 - $1,250.
Counter sign: $200 - $300.

Electric Fan, Sewing Machine
(July 15-21, 1920)

From Oren R. White collection.

Values: $750 - $1,000.

Hunter, Charging Grizzly
(July 22-28, 1920)

From Tom Webster collection. Photo by D. Kowalski. Small counter sign measures 8 1/2" wide x 10 1/2" high; from Tim Melcher collection. Photo by TIM.

Values: $2,750 - $3,000.
Counter sign: $600 - $800.

Good Toilet Equipment
(July 29 - August 4, 1920)

From Oren R. White collection.

Values: $750 - $1,000.

General Utility Oil
(August 5-11, 1920)

From Oren R. White collection. Small counter sign measures 8 1/2" wide x 10 1/2" high; from Tim Melcher collection. Photo by TIM.

Values: $750 - $1,000.
Counter sign: $200 - $300.

Canning and Preserving
(August 12-18, 1920)

From Oren R. White collection.

Values: $750 - $1,000.

Father and Son Cleaning Guns
(August 19-25, 1920)

From Oren R. White collection. Small counter sign measures 8 1/2" wide x 10 1/2" high; from Tim Melcher collection. Photo by TIM.

Values: $2,250 - $2,500.
Counter sign: $500 - $600.

Fall and Winter School Supplies
(August 26 - September 1, 1920)

From Oren R. White collection.

Values: $1,000 - $1,250.

Knives Keep Sharp
(September 2-8, 1920)

From Oren R. White collection.

Values: $750 - $1,000.

Boy Scout Building Farm Fence
(September 9-15, 1920)

From Oren R. White collection.

Values: $1,250 - $1,500.

Duck Hunting with Spaniel
(September 16-22, 1920)

From Tim Melcher collection. Small counter sign measures 8 1/2" wide x 10 1/2" high. All photos by TIM.

Values: $2,750 - $3,000.
Counter sign: $500 - $600.

Housecleaning
(September 23-29, 1920)

The last of the one-sided sets. From Oren R. White collection.

Values: $750 - $1,000.

Tools and Workbench
(September 30 - October 6, 1920)

Small counter sign from Tim Melcher collection; photo by TIM. It measures 8 1/2" wide x 10 1/2" high.

Values - Counter sign: $200 - $300.

A few good mechanic's tools are better than a whole kit of poor ones
Buy
WINCHESTER TOOLS

Extinguish Fire
(October 7-13, 1920)

First of the two-sided sets. (For the remainder of the chapter, the front and back sides of a set will be on the same page.) From Tom Webster collection. Photos by D. Kowalski.

Values: $1,500 - $1,750.

Duck Hunting from Boat
(October 14-20, 1920)

Stoves and Heaters
(October 21-27, 1920)

Two-sided set. From Tom Webster collection. Photos by D. Kowalski.

Values: $3,750 - $4,000.

Scissors
(October 28 - November 3, 1920)

Brown sepia tone.

Cooking Utensils
(November 4-10, 1920)

Two-sided set. From Oren R. White collection.

Values: $1,500 - $1,750.

Goose Hunting
(November 11-17, 1920)

Small counter sign from Tim Melcher collection; photo by TIM. It measures 8 1/2" wide x 10 1/2" high.

Values - Counter sign: $600 - $800.

Thanksgiving Turkey
(November 18-24, 1920)

Two-sided set. From Tom Webster collection. Photos by D. Kowalski.

Values: $3,750 - $4,000.

Ice Skating
(November 25 - December 1, 1920)

Wrapping Christmas Gifts
(December 2-8, 1920)

Two-sided set. From Oren R. White collection.

Values: $1,750 - $2,000.

Mom and Dad Wrapping Gifts
(December 9-15, 1920)

Model 12 shotgun on chair.

Christmas Morning Family Scene
(December 16-25, 1920)

Two-sided set. From Oren R. White collection.

Values: $2,000 - $2,250.

Winchester Junior Rifle Corps at Shooting Gallery
(December 26 - January 5, 1921)

Kitchen Knife
(January 6-12, 1921)

Brown sepia tone. Two-sided set. From Oren R. White collection.

Values: $3,750 - $4,000.

Skating with Sled
(January 13-19, 1921)

Kitchen Knife
(January 20-26, 1921)

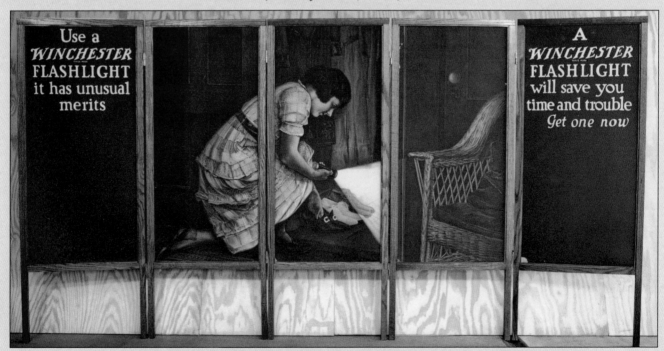

Brown sepia tone. Two-sided set. From Oren R. White collection.

Values: $1,500 - $1,750.

Repairing Wagon
(March 3-9; June 23-29; September 29 - October 5, 1921)

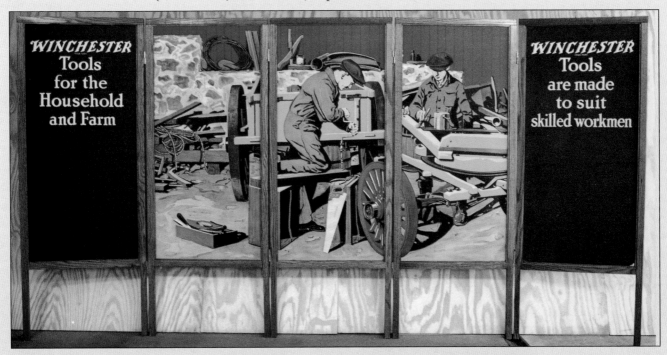

Each side of a set is now typically scheduled for multiple weeks during the year.

Kitchen and Butcher Knives
(April 21-27; October 27 - November 2, 1921)

Two-sided set. From Oren R. White collection.

Values: $1,750 - $2,000.

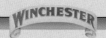

Flashlight, Changing Tire
(March 10-16, 1921)

Brown sepia tone.

Poultry Yard
(March 24-30, 1921)

Two-sided set. From Tom Webster collection. Photos by D. Kowalski.

Values: $1,500 - $1,750.

Winchester Junior Rifle Corps, Learn to Shoot
(March 17-23, 1921; December 26 - January 4, 1922)

Fly Fishing
(March 31 - April 6; June 2-9; August 18-24, 1921)

Brown sepia tone. Two-sided set. From Tom Webster collection. Photos by D. Kowalski.

Values: $3,750 - $4,000.

Roller Skating with Tricycle
(April 7-13, 1921)

Brown sepia tone.

House Cleaning, Painting
(April 14-20, 1921)

Brown sepia tone. Two-sided set. From Tom Webster collection. Photos by D. Kowalski.

Values: $1,500 - $1,750.

Better Trapshooting
(May 12-18; June 9-15, 1921)

A Handy Light
(May 26 - June 1: July 7-13; October 6-12, 1921)

Two-sided set. From Tom Webster collection. Photos by D. Kowalski.

Values: $3,750 - $4,000.

Canning, Paring Knives
(August 11-17; September 1-7, 1921)

Brown sepia tone.

Grouse Hunting
(September 15-21; November 10-16, 1921)

Two-sided set. From Tom Webster collection. Photos by D. Kowalski.

Values: $3,000 - $3,250.

Spatula and Knives
(January 5-11; February 16-22, 1922)

Panels one and five were left blank so retailers could hang products on the frame or build displays in front of the blank panel.

Five Flashlight Scenes
(January 19-25, 1922)

Two-sided set. From Oren R. White collection.

Values: $1,500 - $1,750.

Shaving Razors
(February 2-8, 1922)

Panels one and five again left blank; both sides on this set.

Metal and Carpentry Tools
(March 2-8; April 27 - May 3, 1922)

Two-sided set. From Oren R. White collection.

Values: $1,500 - $1,750.

Flashlights, Auto Accessories
(March 9-15; May 25-31, 1922)

Winchester Junior Rifle Corps, .22 rifles
(March 16-22, 1922)

Two-sided set. From Tom Webster collection. Photos by D. Kowalski.

Values: $3,750 - $4,000.

Fly Fishing, Tackle
(March 23-29, 1922)

Seeds and Garden Tools
(March 30 - April 5, 1922)

Although we have no evidence that Winchester sold its own garden seeds, it supported seed sales. Similarly, it didn't sell garden hose, electric vacuum cleaners or ice cream freezers until 1926 or 1927, but we still see them pictured in earlier five-panel sets. Two-sided set. From Oren R. White collection.

Values: $2,750 - $3,000.

Boys Roller Skating
(April 6-12, 1922)

Paint, Cleaning Supplies
(April 13-19, 1922)

Two-sided set. From Tom Webster collection. Photos by D. Kowalski.

Values: $1,750 - $2,000.

Baseball Products
(April 20-26, 1922)

An unusual black sepia tone print, instead of the typical brown.

Five Cutlery Scenes
(May 4-10, 1922)

Two-sided set. From Oren R. White collection.

Values: $3,250 - $3,500.

Champion Trapshooters
(May 11-17, 1922)

Another sepia tone print, back to brown.

Vacation Goods
(June 1-7; July 20-26, 1922)

Two-sided set. From Oren R. White collection.

Values: $3,750 - $4,000.

Electrical Appliances
(June 15-21; July 6-12, 1922)

A rare advertising image of a now-rare toaster and equally rare coffee pot.

Carpentry Tools
(June 22-28, 1922)

Two-sided set. From Oren R. White collection.

Values: $1,500 - $1,750.

Flashlights
(July 13-19; August 17-23, 1922)

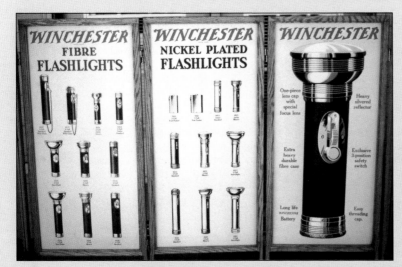

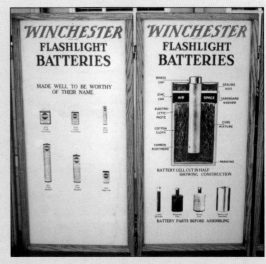

Rifles and Ammunition
(August 3-9, 1922)

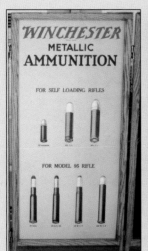

Two-sided set. From Tim Melcher collection. Photos by TIM.

Values: $3,500 - $3,750.

Sports Equipment
(September 7-13, 1922)

Several rare balls shown. Individual panels with the "Winchester" name on them often got separated from the full set because of a special subject.

Shotguns and Shells
(September 14-20, 1922)

Two-sided set. From Oren R. White collection.

Values: $3,750 - $4,000.

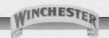

Axes and Saws
(September 21-27, 1922)

Multiple Tools
(September 28 - October 4, 1922)

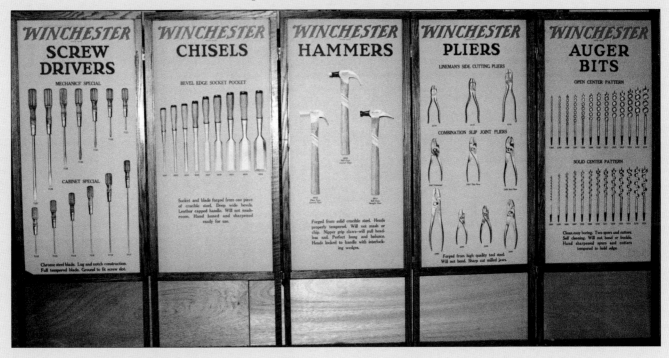

Two-sided set. From Oren R. White collection.

Values: $2,250 - $2,500.

Two Duck Hunters
(October 12-18, 1922)

Multiple Tools
(October 19-25, 1922)

Two-sided set. From Tom Webster collection. Photos by D. Kowalski.

Values: $3,750 - $4,000.

Five Ice Skating Scenes
(January 11-17, 1923)

Basketball
(January 25-31, 1923)

From Oren R. White collection.

Values: $3,750 - $4,000.

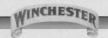

Five Flashlight Scenes
(February 8-14, 1923)

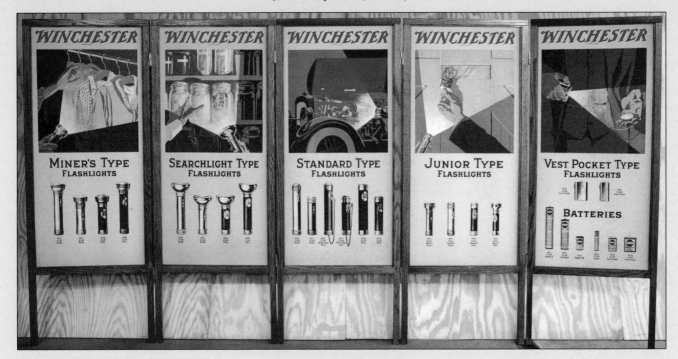

Five Tool Scenes
(March 1-7, 1923)

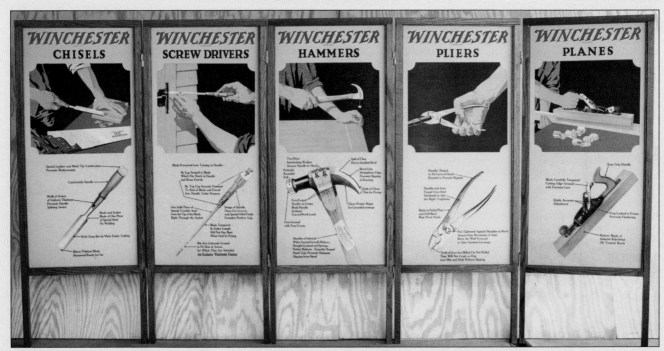

Two-sided set. From Oren R. White collection.

Values: $1,750 - $2,000.

Fishing Tackle
(March 15-21, 1923)

Baseball
(March 29 - April 4; May 24-30, 1923)

Two-sided set. From Tom Webster collection. Photos by D. Kowalski.

Values: $3,750 - $4,000.

Winchester Junior Rifle Corps at Range
(April 5-11; May 3-9, 1923)

Five Tool Scenes
(Dates not available, Summer 1923)

Two-sided set. From Oren R. White collection.

Values: $3,750 - $4,000.

Five Tool Scenes
(April 26 - May 2; May 31 - June 6, 1923)

Fishing Tackle
(May 10-16, 1923)

Two-sided set. From Tom Webster collection. Photos by D. Kowalski.

Values: $3,750 - $4,000.

Large Football and Equipment
(September 13-19, 1923)

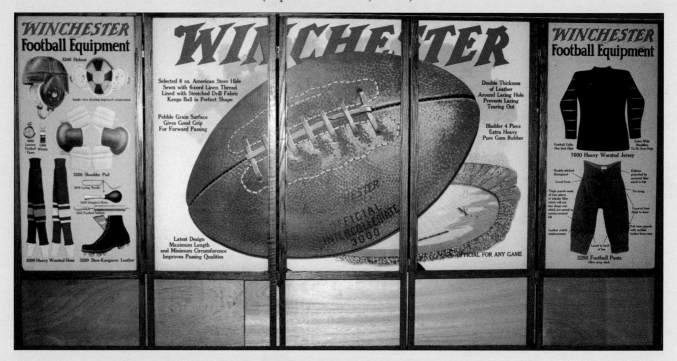

Cutaway Shotshell
(September 20-26, 1923)

Two-sided set. From Oren R. White collection.

Values: $3,750 - $4,000.

Large Focusing Flashlight
(October 4-10, 1923)

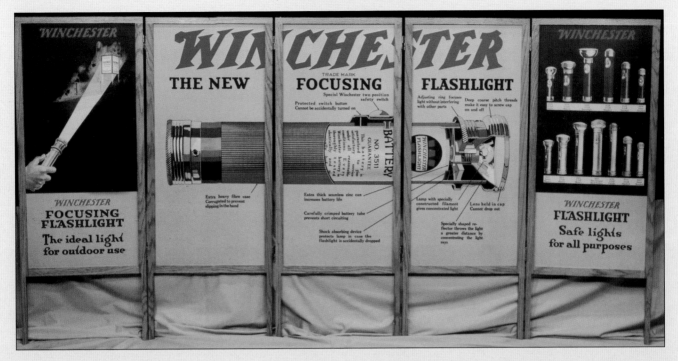

Multiple Tools
(October 25-31, 1923)

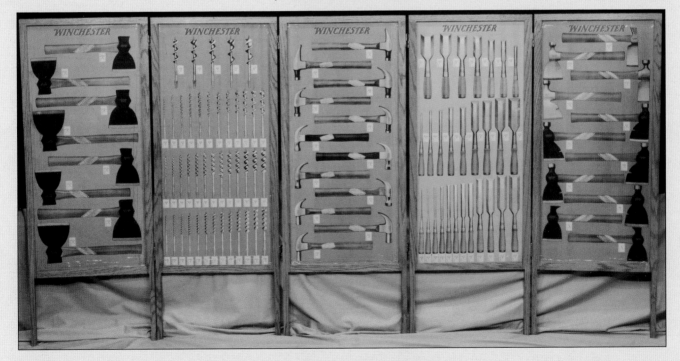

Two-sided set. From Tom Webster collection. Photos by D. Kowalski.

Values: $1,750 - $2,000.

Multiple Tools
(November 15-21, 1923)

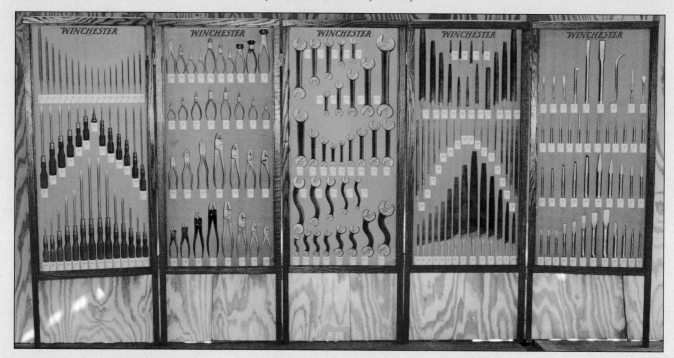

Winchester Store Christmas
(December 6-26, 1923)

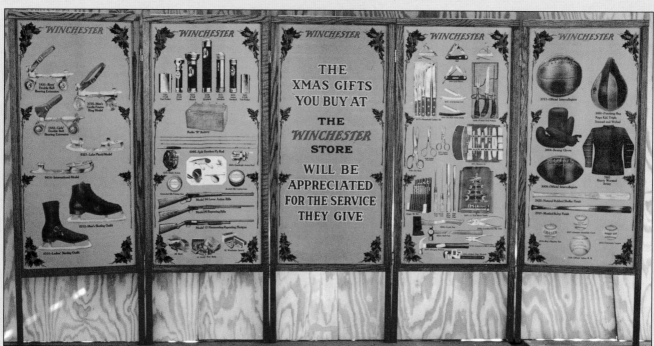

Two-sided set. From Oren R. White collection.

Values: $3,500 - $3,750.

Multiple Cutlery
(January 3-9, 1924)

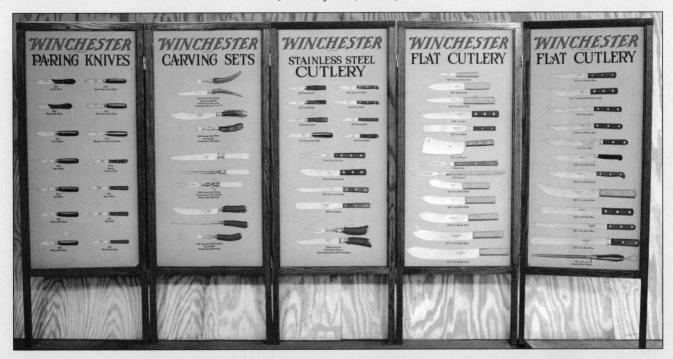

Large Pipe Wrench
(February 28 - March 5, 1924)

Two-sided set. From Oren R. White collection.

Values: $1,750 - $2,000.

Steel Goods
(March 13-19, 1924)

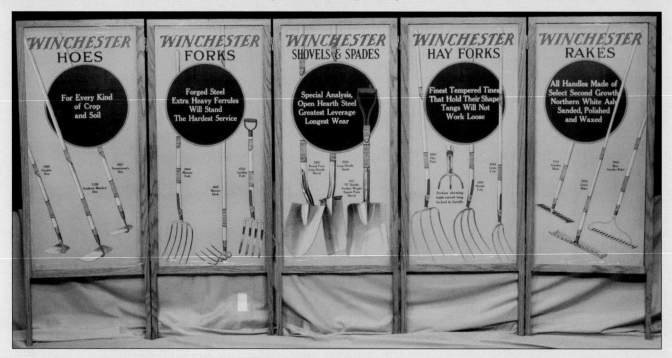

Split Bamboo Rods
(March 20-26, 1924)

Two-sided set. From Tom Webster collection. Photos by D. Kowalski.

Values: $3,000 - $3,250.

Large Paint Can
(April 10-16, 1924)

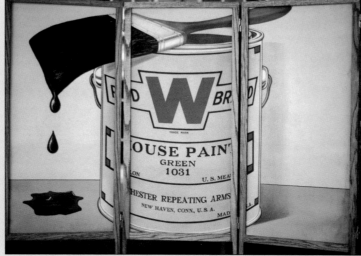

Large Hand Saw
(April 24-30, 1924)

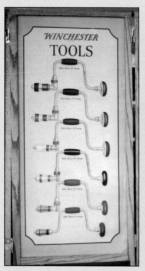

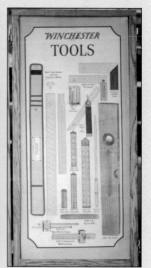

Two-sided set. From Tim Melcher collection. Photos by TIM.

Values: $3,500 - $3,750.

Baseball Goods
(May 1-7, 1924)

Vacation Needs
(June 5-11, 1924)

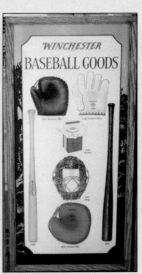

Two-sided set. From Tim Melcher collection. Photos by TIM.

Values: $3,750 - $4,000.

Garden Implements
(Summer, 1924)

Paint and Varnish
(Summer, 1924)

Two-sided set. From Oren R. White collection.

Values: $1,750 - $2,000.

Summer Sports
(May, 1926)

Large Scissors
(June, 1926)

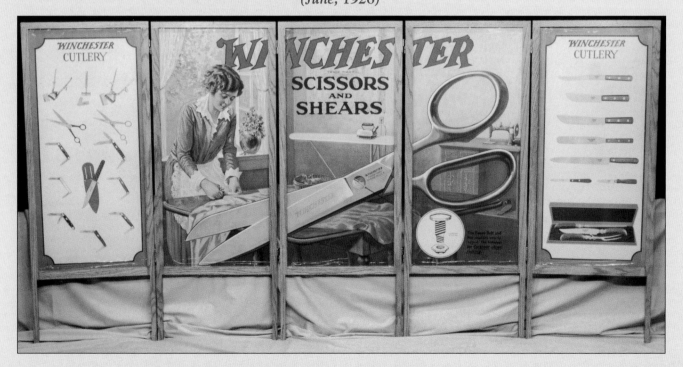

Two-sided set. From Tom Webster collection. Photos by D. Kowalski.

Values: $3,500 - $3,750.

School Days, Football
(September, 1926)

Flashlights and Batteries
(October, 1926)

Two-sided set. From Oren R. White collection.

Values: $3,000 - $3,250.

Family Thanksgiving
(November, 1926)

Christmas Gifts Under Tree
(December, 1926)

Two-sided set. From Tim Melcher collection. Photos by TIM.

Values: $3,750 - $4,000.

When a Feller Needs a Friend - Comedy
(January, 1928)

Scene painted by Briggs.

Out on a Plank - Comedy
(February, 1928)

Scene painted by F. Fox. Two-sided set. From Tom Webster collection. Photos by D. Kowalski.

Values: $3,750 - $4,000.

Garden Scene - Comedy
(March, 1928)

Scene painted by Briggs.

Baseball - Comedy
(April, 1928)

Scene painted by F. Fox. Two-sided set. From Oren R. White collection.

Values: $3,000 - $3,250.

Roller Skating - Comedy
(May, 1928)

Scene painted by F. Fox.

Kitchen Cutlery - Comedy
(June, 1928)

Scene painted by F. Fox. Two-sided set. From Oren R. White collection.

Values: $3,000 - $3,250.

Winchester Store (Lilliputians) - Comedy
(July, 1928)

Scene painted by Winsor McKay.

The Way to a Man's Heart - Comedy
(August, 1928)

Scene painted by Briggs. Two-sided set. From Oren R. White collection.

Values: $3,000 - $3,250.

Thanksgiving - Comedy
(November, 1928)

Scene painted by Briggs.

Christmas Gifts Under Tree
(December, 1928)

  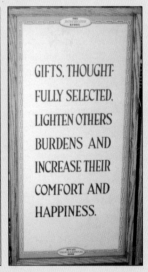

Panel with bright star says, "There came wise men from the East carrying gifts." Two-sided set. From Tim Melcher collection. Photos by TIM.

Values: $3,000 - $3,250.

Two–Sided Counter Signs

Bang!; Fishing Tackle

WJRC - keen-eyed boys; Mechanic Tools

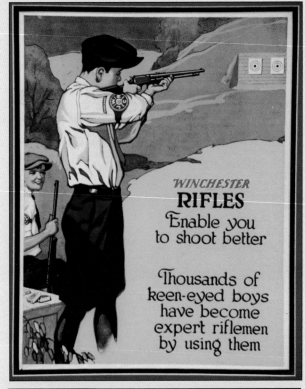

Image size is 10 1/2" wide x 13 1/2" high; the largest of three sizes. From Tom Webster collection. Photos by D. Kowalski.

Image size is 10 1/2" wide x 13 1/2" high. From Tom Webster collection. Photos by D. Kowalski.

Values: $2,500 - $2,750.

Values: $2,500 - $2,750.

WJRC Matches; Tools

Boys Roller Skating; Kitchen Knives

Image size is 10 1/2" wide x 13 1/2" high. From T. Webster collection. Photos by D. Kowalski.

Values: $2,500 - $2,750.

Image size is 10 1/2" wide x 13 1/2" high. From T. Webster collection. Photos by D. Kowalski.

Values: $700 - $800.

Roller Skating; House Paint

Man and Woman Fishing; Bride, Carving Set

Image size is 10 1/2" wide x 13 1/2" high. From Tom Webster collection. Photos by D. Kowalski.

Image size is 10 1/2" wide x 13 1/2" high. From Tom Webster collection. Photos by D. Kowalski.

Values: $300 - $400.

Values: $500 - $600.

Scout Axe; Scissors and Shears

WJRC - Kneeling Position: WJRC - Sitting Position (Fronts of two signs)

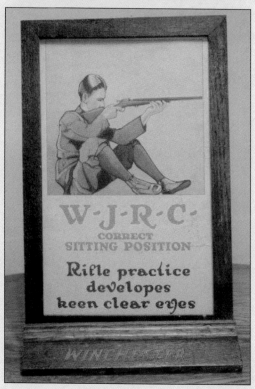

Image size is 6 1/2" wide x 10" high; the middle size of three sizes. From Tom Webster collection. Photos by D. Kowalski.

Image size is 6 1/2" wide x 10" high. From Jennifer Hunter and Gary Gole collection. Photos by J. Hunter and G. Gole.

Values: $800 - $1,000.

Values: $2,000 - $2,500 (either version).

Pull!; Steel Bait Casting Rods

Dead Bird!; Flashlight and Fuse Box

Image size is 6 1/2" wide x 10" high. From Tom Webster collection. Photos by D. Kowalski.

Image size is 6 1/2" wide x 10" high. From Don Alters collection. Photos by D. Alters.

Values: $800 - $1,000.

Values: $800 - $1,000.

Repeater Shells; Multiple Action Reels

Winter Fuel; Nail Hammer Special

Image size is 6 1/2" wide x 10" high. From Tom Webster collection. Photos by D. Kowalski.

Values: $800 - $1,000.

Image size is 6 1/2" wide x 10" high. From Don Alters collection. Photos by D. Alters.

Values: $500 - $700.

Baseball Goods; Monkey Wrenches

Punching Bags; A World's Record

Image size is 6 1/2" wide x 10" high. From Tom Webster collection. Photos by D. Kowalski.

Values: $700 - $800.

Image size is 6 1/2" wide x 10" high. From Tom Turigliatti collection. Photos by T. Turigliatti.

Values: $800 - $1,000.

Auto Tool Kits; Perfect Bearings, Roller Skates

Right After It!; General Utility Oil

Image size is 6 1/2" wide x 10" high. From Tom Webster collection. Photos by D. Kowalski.

Image size is 5 1/2" wide x 7" high. A rare piece in the smallest size. From Tom Webster collection. Photos by D. Kowalski.

Values: $300 - $400.

Values: $400 - $500.

Dead Bird!; Bass Flies

Hand Trap; Plug Bait

Image size is 5 1/2" wide x 7" high. From Tom Webster collection. Photos by D. Kowalski.

Image size is 5 1/2" wide x 7" high. From Tom Webster collection. Photos by D. Kowalski.

Values: $400 - $500.

Values: $400 - $500.

Punches and Cold Chisels; Metal Preparations

Scout Knife; Screw Drivers

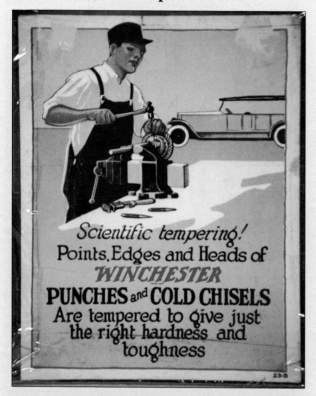

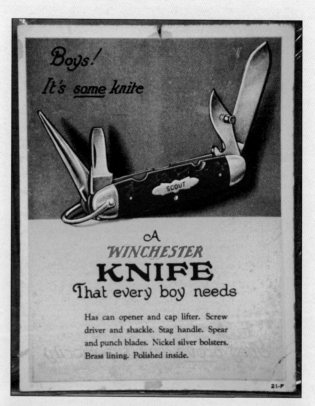

Image size is 5 1/2" wide x 7" high. From Tom Webster collection. Photos by D. Kowalski.

Values: $250 - $300.

Image size is 5 1/2" wide x 7" high. From Tom Webster collection. Photos by D. Kowalski.

Values: $250 - $300.

Auto Enamel; Scooter

Pocket Knives; Rakes

Image size is 5 1/2" wide x 7" high. Scooter images are rare in Winchester advertising. From Tom Webster collection. Photos by D. Kowalski.

Values: $250 - $300.

Image size is 5 1/2" wide x 7" high. From Tom Webster collection. Photos by D. Kowalski.

Values: $150 - $200.

Wood Saws; (Roller Skates on back - not shown)

Image size is 6 1/2" wide x 10" high. From Don Alters collection. Photos by D. Alters.

Values: $300 - $350.

Hunter's Pattern Axe; (Buy School Supplies on back - not shown)

Image size is 6 1/2" wide x 10" high. From Don Alters collection. Photos by D. Alters.

Values: $300 - $350.

Booklets, Brochures and Flyers

The Trap Shooter's Guide (Booklet)

The Trap Shooter's Guide. We lead off this chapter with a booklet probably created in the late 1800s as trapshooting gained popularity in the United States. The stylized tree, the gaudy clothing and the old "blunderbuss" shotguns pictured are not seen in any other Winchester advertising in this volume. Size is 4 1/2" wide x 6 1/2" high. From Tom Webster collection. Photo by D. Kowalski.

Values: $350 - $450.

Shotgun Shell Booklets

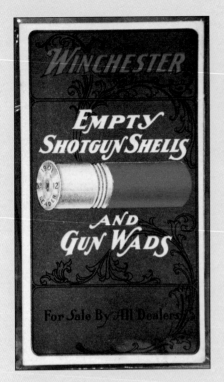
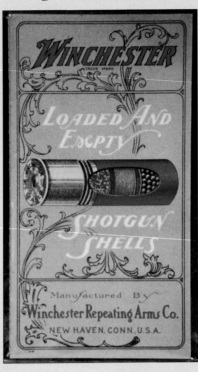
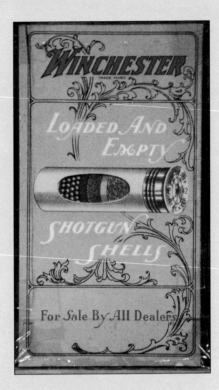

Empty Shotgun Shells and Gun Wads (backside - above) and Loaded and Empty Shotgun Shells (front and back - above) have the same "Winchester" logo as "They Are Hitters" poster from 1904. Each measures 3 3/8" wide x 6 1/8" high. The other Loaded and Empty Shotgun Shells (The W Brand) was probably the next version done about 1906 since it does not yet use the "lightning strike" logo. It is 4" wide x 6 1/4" high. From Tom Webster collection. Photos by D. Kowalski.

Values: $300 - $400 (any of the three versions).

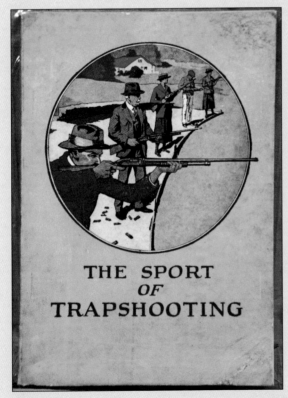

The Sport of Trapshooting (Booklet)

The Sport of Trapshooting. Does not even show the "Winchester" logo on front. This booklet is perfect bound (square-back binding). Size is 4 3/4" wide x 6 7/8" high. From Tom Webster collection. Photo by D. Kowalski.

Values: $150 - $250.

Three Firearms and Ammunition Booklets

Three companion booklets cover .22 caliber rifles, shot guns and high power rifles. The scene on the .22 booklet was used on early Winchester Junior Rifle Corps posters from 1917-1918. Each measures 4 1/8" wide x 6" high. From Tom Webster collection. Photo by D. Kowalski.

Values: $150 - $200 (any version).

Hunting, Fishing & Camping (Booklet)

This Hunting, Fishing & Camping booklet dates from the 1920s. A rare booklet with a rare reference to camping. Size is 6 1/4" wide x 9 1/8" high. From Tom Webster collection. Photo by D. Kowalski.

Values: $700 - $800.

"New Rival" (Brochure)

"New Rival" Loaded Shells Excel. Probably the first New Rival brochure. The New Rival green loaded shells were introduced in 1897. Size (closed) is 3 3/8" wide x 5 3/4" high. From Tom Webster collection. Photo by D. Kowalski.

Values: $350 - $400.

Repeater (Brochure)

Repeater loaded shells were introduced in 1900. This early brochure (closed) measures 3 3/8" wide x 5 3/4" high. From Tom Webster collection. Photo by D. Kowalski.

Values: $300 - $350.

Leader (Brochure)

Leader loaded shells were introduced in 1894. This early brochure probably dates from about 1900; perhaps it was even the companion brochure to the Repeater version above. The experimenting that Winchester designers did with logo typefaces in the late 1890s (noted in the calendar section) really shows here. Logo typefaces are not even the same on the front and back of this brochure. And if you compare them to the Repeater brochure above, you see three very distinct typestyles (all very ornate) on the "Winchester" logo. Designers gone wild, if you will. Size (closed) is 3 3/8" wide x 5 3/4" high. From Tom Webster collection. Photo by D. Kowalski.

Values: $300 - $350.

Repeater, Leader, Nublack (Brochures)

Here's the next generation of shell brochures. All three on this page use the "Winchester" logo typeface we see on the 1904 "The Kind That Gets 'Em" Big Game poster and "The Cock of the Woods" poster from 1905. The Repeater version doesn't yet use the red "W" so it was probably done in 1904-1905. But the other two do show the red "W" adopted in 1906. (The Nublack loaded shells were introduced in 1905.) Each brochure (closed) measures 3 3/8" wide x 5 3/4" high. From Tom Webster collection. Photos by D. Kowalski.

Values: $300 - $350 (versions on this page).

Trapshooting Scorecards

Three Trapshooting Scorecards. The "front" of each is the score-card; the scorecard pictured is the reverse side of the "Loads" version (below), which has a "5-06" date (May, 1906) at the bottom. This is probably the earliest of the three. Each is 3 1/4" wide x 5 1/2" high. From Tom Webster collection. Photos by D. Kowalski.

Values: $300 - $400 (any of these versions).

Shotgun Shells (Fake Book)

Loaded Shotgun Shells. For lack of a better term, we've called this unusual cardboard piece a "fake book." It does not open, just has the front and back sides pictured below. The red "W" dates this as a post-1906 creation. Size is 3 1/2" wide x 6 1/4" high. From Tom Webster collection. Photos by D. Kowalski.

Values: $350 - $450.

Breech Caps (Brochure)

Breech Caps. The red "W" dates this as a post-1906 brochure. The "11-9" at bottom is probably a reference to November, 1909. Size closed is 3 3/8" wide x 5 3/4" high. From Tom Webster collection. Photo by D. Kowalski.

Values: $300 - $400.

Rimfire Cartridges (Brochure)

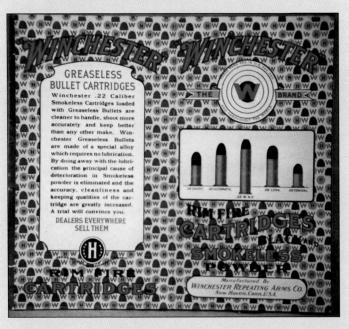

Rimfire Cartridges. A very rare brochure that probably dates from the 1906-1915 era. Size closed is 3 3/8" wide x 5 3/4" high. From Tom Webster collection. Photo by D. Kowalski.

Values: $400 - $500.

Revolver Championship of World
(Brochure)

The Revolver Championship of the World. Winchester produced far less literature on pistols and cartridges than they did on rifles and shotguns. This brochure probably dates from the 1906-1910 era. Size closed is 3 1/2" wide x 6 1/2" high. From Tim Melcher collection. Photo by TIM.

Values: $200 - $300.

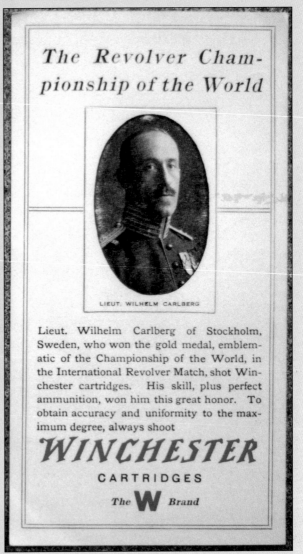

Some Sensible Suggestions
(Christmas Brochure)

A Winchester Store brochure from the 1920s (front/back - above left; inside - left) that promotes a wide range of Christmas gifts. Size closed is 3 1/2" wide x 6 1/4" high. From Tom Webster collection. Photos by D. Kowalski.

Values: $200 - $300.

"The Most Perfect Repeater" the

WINCHESTER

12 GAUGE Model 1912 Shotgun

Model 12 (Brochure)

"The Most Perfect Repeater" brochure (open, showing front and back cover) was probably created in late 1911 or early 1912 for the introduction of the Model 12. Size closed is 6 1/2" wide x 3 5/8" high. From Tim Melcher collection. Photo by TIM.

Values: $200 - $300.

American Boy (Wagon Brochure)

Are you an American Boy? Another "Winchester Store" sales brochure from 1920s (front/back - above right; inside - right) that promotes the (Model WS2) wagon with the box that slides back and off. Size closed is 3 1/2" wide x 6 1/4" high. From Tom Webster collection. Photos by D. Kowalski.

Values: $200 - $300.

WINCHESTER
"BRUSH" SHELLS

SOMETHING NEW FOR FIELD AND BRUSH SHOOTING

Winchester "Brush" Shells help wonderfully to make big bags. With them you can use your duck or trap gun for field shooting and make many kills which otherwise would be misses, without mutilating the game. The most pronounced point of superiority of Winchester "Brush" Shells is that they make an open and uniform pattern at ranges of from 25 to 30 yards when used in a choke bore gun

WITHOUT LOSS OF VELOCITY, PENETRATION OR UNIFORMITY.

In other words—even with increased spread of shot—the velocity and penetration and uniformity remain substantially the same as in shells loaded in the regular way. Winchester "Brush" Shells are loaded with smokeless powder only in either "Leader" or "Repeater" brands but in the following loads only:—

Gauge	Drams Powder or Equivalent	Ounces Shot	Size Shot	"Leader" List price per 1,000	"Repeater" List price per 1,000
12—3 3/4	3	1 1/4	4 to 10 only	$48.50	$37.50
16—2 3-16	2 1/2	1	6 to 10 only	46.00	35.00

FOR SALE BY ALL DEALERS

WINCHESTER SHELLS WON ALL THE SHOOTING HONORS IN 1905 AND THE GRAND AMERICAN HANDICAP IN 1906.

WINCHESTER
"BRUSH" Shotgun Shells

They make cylinder bore patterns in choke bore guns WITHOUT LOSS OF VELOCITY, PENETRATION or UNIFORMITY, and help wonderfully to make big bags.

Look for the **W** on Every Box

"Brush" Shotshells (Brochures)

"Brush" Shotshells. Two brochures (above and above left) helped introduce "Brush" shells in 1905. The brochure on left (inside view) pictures a Leader shell but Winchester launched the Brush shell in both Repeater and Leader brands in 1905, then in Ranger in 1925. Left brochure is dated 1-8-6 (January 8, 1906) and right one dated 9-11 (September 1911). Copy on the open brochure on left also contains the phrase "help wonderfully to make big bags" - a phrase so unique it could only have been done by the same copywriter who wrote the closed version on the right. Sizes closed are approximately 4" wide x 8 1/2" high. From Tim Melcher collection. Photos by TIM.

Values: $200 - $300.

Repeater Speed Loads (Flyer)

Repeater Speed Loads. Flyer on light paper may have been sent to retailers as part of a regular information packet. Repeater Speed Loads were introduced in 1927 and discontinued in 1932. Size is 17" wide x 23" high. From Tom Turigliatti collection. Photo by T. Turigliatti.

Values: $250 - $300.

Envelopes

Bearded Hunter, Model 86

Available in both this four-color version and a black-and-white version. Probably a pre-1900 design. Postmark - 1908. In general, the most valuable envelopes have postmarks; in fact, some collectors will not buy them without postmarks.

Values: $150 - $200 (color); $100 - $150 (b/w).

Backside from Pre-1907

All envelopes had significant advertising copy and/or line drawings on the backside. Before 1907, envelopes did not have the big "W" or "Winchester" in "lightning strike" logo typeface. Envelopes measure 6 1/2" wide x 3 5/8" high.

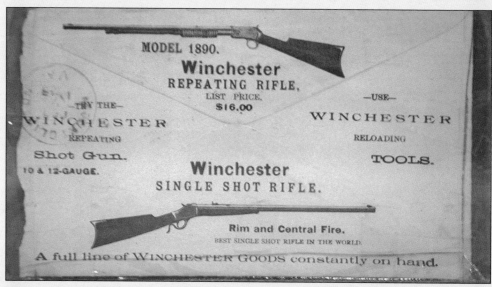

Backside from Post-1907

This is typical copy on envelopes created after 1907. While there are some small variations, this one illustrates the use of the red "W" and the "lightning strike" logo. This extended patent line was typical on many Winchester products and shell boxes from about 1912-1916.

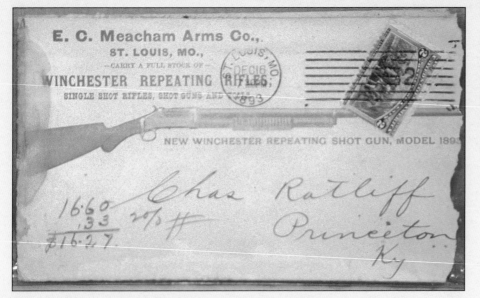

Note: The pre-1900 envelopes (left) possibly were each produced in red, blue, or black ink versions. Red ink is most common; blue fairly rare; black very rare (versions in black ink would be valued at $250-$300).

Model 93 (red)

The Model 93 was the first slide-action repeating shotgun Winchester built. Postmark - 1893.

Values: $150 - $200 (red).

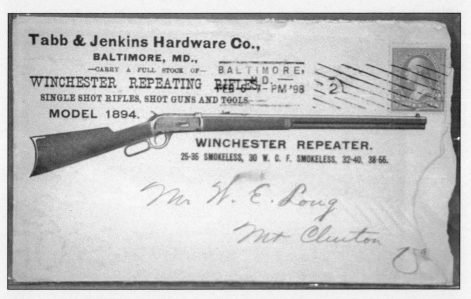

Model 94 (blue)

The Model 94 - the gun that won the West. Postmark - 1898.

Values: $200 - $250 (blue).

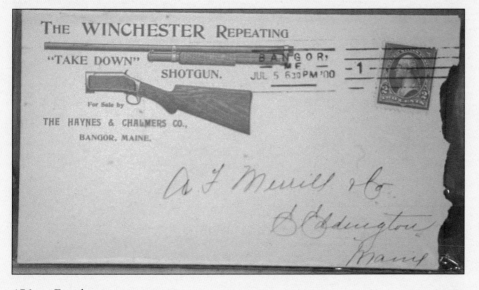

Model 97 (red)

The Model 97 was Winchester's first "takedown" shotgun. The 12 gauge was available in either solid or takedown styles. The 16 gauge only came as a takedown. Postmark - 1900.

Values: $150 - $200 (red).

Hanging Ducks

Shows a "lightning strike" Winchester logo with an exaggerated initial "W." Created in 1906-1910 era. Postmark - 1910.

Values:
$100 - $200.

Dawn of the Open Season

That was the name of this scene from the 1910 poster reportedly painted by N.C. Wyeth. Postmark - year not readable.

Values:
$100 - $200.

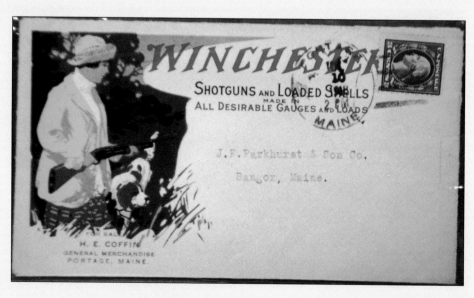

Woman in Yellow Coat

Image is from poster done in 1911 or 1912. Postmark - 1918.

Values:
$300 - $400.

Hunter with Model 12

Robert Robinson painted this picture for the 1913 calendar. Not postmarked (but Tom Webster reports he just purchased a postmarked copy).

Values:
$300 - $400.

Hunter and Guide on Rock

Image is on the long point-of-purchase window display produced in the 1914-1916 time frame. Postmark - 1918.

Values:
$300 - $400.

Hunter on Snowshoes

Philip R. Goodwin's painting from his 1906 poster. (We took this envelope and the following three out of our general sequence because we wanted to group the Goodwin envelopes together.) Postmark - 1914.

Values:
$300 - $400.

Bear Coming Out of Cabin

Philip R. Goodwin's painting from his 1909 poster. The retailer in Panama who used these obviously kept his supply for several years. Postmark - 1928.

Values:
$300 - $400.

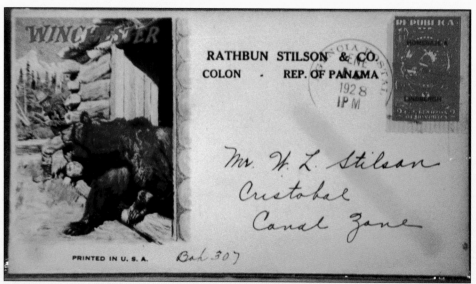

Two Hunters at Camp

A 1914 Window Display featured this painting by Philip R. Goodwin. Postmark - 1917.

Values:
$300 - $400.

Two Hunters and Airedale Terrier

Philip R. Goodwin created this scene for the 1916 calendar. It is not a particularly rare envelope. Postmark - 1918.

Values:
$150 - $250.

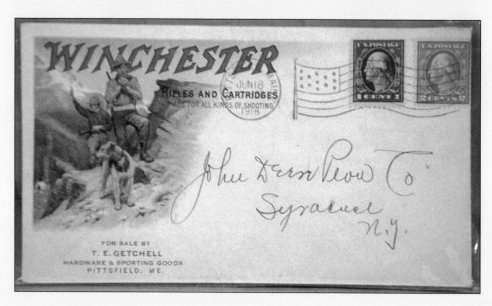

Counter Pads

The Celebrated ...

This may be the only design/color like it still in existence. Possibly pre-1900 design. Size is 13 3/8" wide x 10 3/8" high.

Values: $400 - $500.

The Celebrated ...

Size is 12 5/8" wide x 10 3/8" high.

Values: $300 - $400.

The Celebrated ...

Size is 13 5/8" wide x 11 1/8" high.

Values: $200 - $300.

Note: All counter pads are heavy felt (subject to shrinkage or possible stretching). All examples from Tom Webster collection. Photos by D. Kowalski.

The Celebrated ...

Outlined letters. Size is 12 5/8" wide x 9 1/2" high.

Values: $250 - $300.

The Celebrated ...

Outlined letters. Size is 13 7/8" wide x 10 5/8" high.

Values: $300 - $400.

The Celebrated ...

Structural damage (and possible shrinkage) caused by dry cleaning. May be the same version as the one opposite (bottom). Size is 13 3/8" wide x 10 7/8" high.

Values: $200 - $300.

Always Use ...

Any counter pad with all red type is very rare. Size is 13 1/4" wide x 10 5/8" high.

Values: $400 - $500.

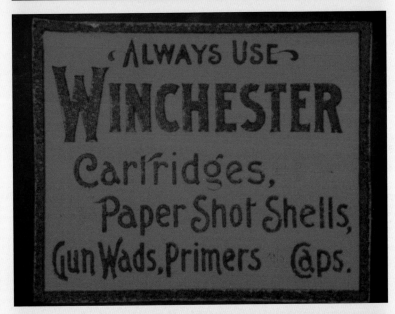

Always Use ...

More common than above example. Size is 13 5/8" wide x 11" high.

Values: $200 - $300.

Always Use ...

Same as above but showing effects of shrinking, stretching and damage to the fabric. Size is 12 7/8" wide x 11 1/8" high.

Values: $200 - $300.

Try The New Rival ...

Early New Rival version. Size is 13 3/4" wide x 11 1/8" high.

Values: $300 - $400.

New Rival ...

Later New Rival version. Size is 12 7/8" wide x 11 1/8" high.

Values: $300 - $400.

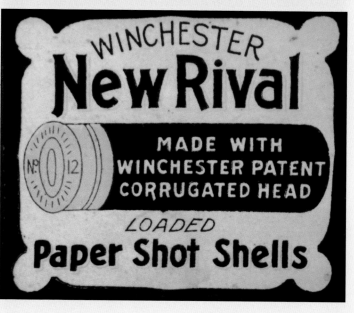

New Rival ...

Later New Rival version. Size is 13 1/8" wide x 11 1/2" high.

Values: $300 - $400.

.22 Cal. Rim Fire Cartridges ...

Fairly rare version. Size is 13 1/4" wide x 11 1/8" high.

Values: $500 - $600.

When Buying Cartridges ...

Big red "W" dates this pad at 1907 or later. Size is 13" wide x 11 1/8" high.

Values: $300 - $400.

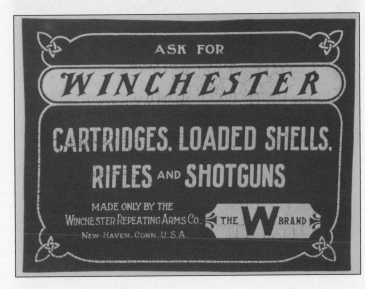

Ask For ...

The largest of the counter pads and the most common one. The big red "W" also dates this at 1907 or later. Size is 15 1/2" wide x 11 1/2" high.

Values: $200 - $300.

The Winchester Junior Rifle Corps (WJRC)

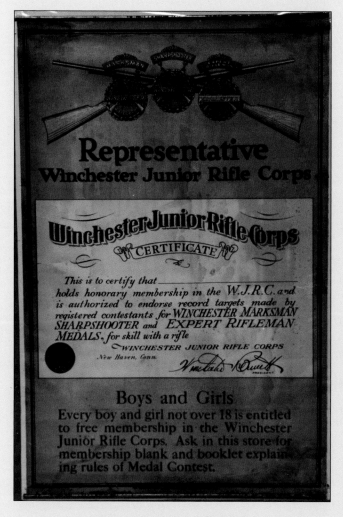

Representative (Poster)

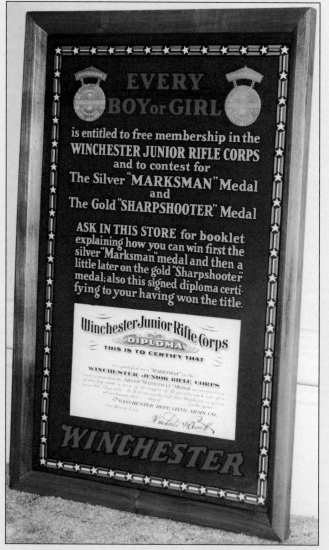

Every Boy or Girl - Membership Poster

Representative. Poster probably created very early in the 1920s to hang in Winchester retail stores. While the early WJRC magazine ads (see page 203, for example) talked only about the silver "Marksman" and gold "Sharpshooter" medals, this poster also illustrates the "Expert Rifleman" medal that was added later in the program. Very few of these Representative posters have been found. It has metal bands top and bottom and measures 12 1/2" wide x 19 1/8" high. From Tom Webster collection. Photo by D. Kowalski.

Values: $1,700 - $2,000.

Every Boy or Girl entitled to free membership. The Winchester Junior Rifle Corps was launched in July, 1917 (first detailed in Sales Department Bulletin No. 84 - July 10, 1917). It lasted until 1924 when the National Rifle Association (NRA) took over the program. Winchester, however, continued to sell the WJRC Range Kits until the end of the 1920s. We also included several WJRC five-panel displays and posters in those sections of the book. This membership poster is extremely rare. It measures 13" wide x 21 1/2" high. From Don Alters collection. Photo by D. Alters.

Values: $2,500 - $2,800.

Boys, Learn to Shoot!; Learn to Shoot Right! - Counter Signs

Boys, learn to shoot! (left). Photo shows a Boy Scout camp. WJRC maintained a strong relationship with the Boy Scouts. A companion sign (facing page), "Learn to shoot right!" shows both young boys and girls getting shooting instructions. Both cardboard signs have easel backs. Created about 1921. Each measures 14 1/8" wide x 10 7/8" high. From Jennifer Hunter and Gary Gole collection. Photo by J. Hunter and G. Gole.

Values: $1,700 - $1,900 (either version).

WJRC Belt

WJRC Belt. A small, cheap belt that often got thrown away, perhaps because "WJRC" wasn't always mentally connected to Winchester. Very few have been found. One-inch-wide woven fiber. From Tom Webster collection. Photo by D. Kowalski.

Values: $2,000 - $2,500.

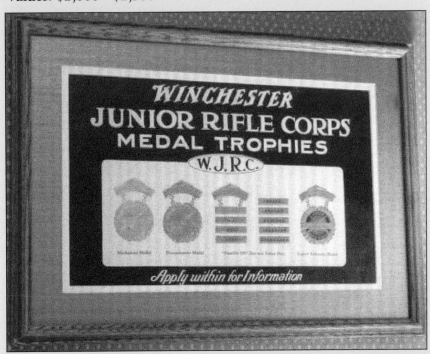

WJRC Medal Trophies - Counter Sign

WJRC Medal Trophies. Cardboard counter sign is one of the few ever found. Shows awards that could be won in WJRC shooting competitions including Marksman, Sharpshooter and Expert Rifleman medals. Produced about 1922. Measures 11" wide x 7 7/8" high. From Jennifer Hunter and Gary Gole collection. Photo by J. Hunter and G. Gole.

Values: $1,800 - $2,000.

1925 National Plaque -
Boy Scout Division

National Shooting Competition Plaque -
1925. WJRC apparently sponsored a special
Boy Scout division at its 1925 match. Plate
reads: WJRC Class 'D' Match - National
Boy Scout - Won by Unit 2654 -
Newtonville, Mass.(achusetts) - March -
1925." Size is 12 1/2" wide x 15" high. From
Tom Webster collection. Photo by D.
Kowalski.

Values: $2,500 - $3,000.

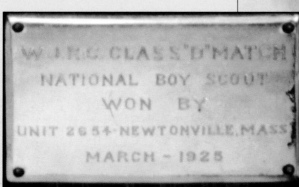

Rules of The Winchester Junior Rifle Corps

Rules. Four versions were created. They're arranged in order with the earliest on the left. Version on left is a "fold-out" design. Second one (red) measures 5 3/4" wide x 3 1/4" high. Third one (blue) is 5 1/2" wide x 3 1/2" wide. Last version (gray cover with no photo) is 5 1/2" wide x 3 1/4" high. Earliest one from Jennifer Hunter and Gary Gole collection. Photo by J. Hunter and G. Gole. Other three from T. Webster collection. Photos by Tom Webster.

Values: (l-r) $150 - $200; $150 - $200; $100 - $150; $100 - $150.

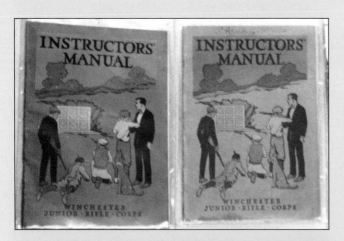

Instructors' Manual

Instructors' Manual. Three versions exist. The earliest one is green (on the far left); the second one is next to it and has a blue panel at the top. Each is 7" wide x 5" high. The final version (not pictured) does not have a photograph on the cover and is similar in design to the final "Rules" book. From T. Webster collection. Photo by Tom Webster.

Values: (1st) $200 - $250; (2nd) $250 - $300; (final version) $150 - $200.

Rifle Safety Booklets

How To Handle a Rifle Safely, Ask Dad For a Rifle. Booklets from the 1920s added to the general marketing effort to get the Winchester name in front of the young men and women of rural America, particularly. The Junior Rifle Corps was only part of that total effort. "How To Handle" measures 3 1/2" wide x 6 1/4" high; "Ask Dad" is 3 1/2" wide x 6 3/8" high. From Tom Webster collection. Photo by D. Kowalski.

Values: $200 - $250 (either one).

The Winchester Store Era

The end of World War I marked a new beginning for Winchester. Hungry for revenues and new markets, they purchased eight manufacturers of hardware, knives and sporting goods in 1919. And kept on buying companies into the early 1920s.

They built their retailer network to 3,400 stores by 1920. Then decided to open their own "Winchester Stores." The urge to wallpaper the country with "Winchester Store" signs prompted them to merge with the Associated Simmons Hardware Company in August, 1922, giving them nationwide distribution into an eventual 6,500 stores, all soon identified as "Winchester Stores." Total products distributed exceeded 5,000 line items detailed in the 1927 catalog.

But it was too much, too fast. The financially strapped Winchester raced headlong into the Great Depression of 1929 by filing bankruptcy. By 1930 the Winchester Store era was over, leaving us a broad range of very collectible products. We present primarily advertising materials from this era and a very select sample of rare products sold.

Enameled Steel Sign

Enameled Steel Sign. Very heavy steel with grommets around six anchor holes. Measures 18" wide x 10 1/8" high. From Tom Webster collection. Photo by D. Kowalski.

Values: $1,400 - $1,700.

Wagon Umbrella

Wagon Umbrella. Has six panels made of heavy canvas with hemmed edges. Each rib is 37 1/4" long. Total height from metal butt cap on bottom of wood handle to tip of rounded wood head cap is 67 1/4". Very few have ever been found. From Tom Webster collection. Photo by D. Kowalski.

Values: $1,200 - $1,500.

GREEN'S HARDWARE & PAINT CO.
THE *WINCHESTER* STORE

Bronze Window Signs

Bronze Window Sign (above). Made of "solid monumental bronze," claims the 1927 Winchester catalog. Has rubber feet and heavy metal easel. Measures 19 1/8" wide x 2 7/8" high. From Tom Webster collection. Photo by D. Kowalski.

Values: $1,400 - $1,700.

Metal Identification Signs

Metal Identification Signs. Winchester made standardized metal identification signs to order (below and below left). The "Schenck" and "Portola" signs are heavy tin with wood frames; they measure 28 1/4" wide x 40 1/2" high. (Dennis Mack also displays pictures of the current Portola Hardware.) Some retailers also created their own metal signs (left). This one is heavy metal and was produced by J.F. Polansky of Caldwell, Texas. It measures 27 1/2" wide x 9 3/4" high. Signs left and below from Tom Webster collection. Photos by D. Kowalski. Sign below left from Dennis Mack collection. Photo by D. Mack.

Values: $700 - $900 (below and below left); $400 - $600 (left).

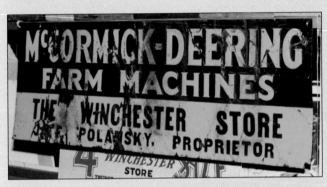

McCORMICK-DEERING FARM MACHINES
THE WINCHESTER STORE
POLANSKY, PROPRIETOR

PORTOLA HARDWARE STORE
PORTOLA · CALIFORNIA
HARDWARE
SPORTING GOODS
THE
WINCHESTER
STORE

SCHENCK MFG. & SUPPLY CO.
PARKERS LANDING · PA.
HARDWARE
SPORTING GOODS
THE
WINCHESTER
STORE

Cardboard Counter Signs, Wall Signs

Counter Signs. Made of cardboard with easel backs (below and below right). "Appointed" sign (below) measures 10 1/8" wide x 13 3/8" high. "Fishing License" sign is 10 7/8' wide x 14" high. Wall signs (right) do not have easel backs. "The Sportsmen's Headquarters" sign measures 14" wide x 11" high. From Tom Webster collection. Photos by D. Kowalski.

Values: $1,000 - $1,200
(any of these three versions).

Hand Fans (Giveaways)

Hand Fans - Giveaways. Individual stores could choose their own picture and pattern. We have included four examples (one left, one below and two in left column of facing page). The back (below left) would have identification and advertising for the individual store. Sizes typically 7" wide x 8 3/4" high. Fan with the hunting scene is 14 1/4" high from top to end of handle. From Tom Webster collection. Photos by D. Kowalski.

**Values: $200 - $250
(rarer hunting scenes higher).**

Framed Pictures (Giveaways)

Framed Pictures - Giveaways. Individual store promotions might also include indoor thermometers attached to framed pictures (below) or simply just framed pictures (below bottom). From Tom Webster collection. Photos by D. Kowalski.

Values: $350 - $500 (with original frame).

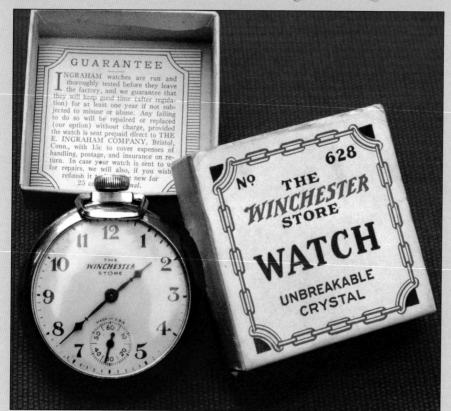

Pocket Watch

A pocket watch with a very rare box variation where the top has thumb cuts and pulls off from above. The more common box design has an inner portion that pulls out of the side of outer sleeve. From Brook Davis collection. Photo by B. Davis.

Values: $1,700 - $2,000 (box and watch; box triples value of watch).

Souvenir Pencils

Box of 20 Souvenir Pencils. Created to look like Winchester cartridges. The only box found to date. From Brook Davis collection. Photo by B. Davis.

Values: $2,000 - $2,500 (full box).

Console Radio

Console Radio. Less than five have ever been found. Size is 50" high x 25" wide x 17" deep. From Tom Webster collection. Photo by T. Webster.

Values: $3,500 - $4,000.

Gas Range

Gas Range. This extremely rare piece has "The Winchester Store" identification in three places. The only one found to date. Size is 46 1/2" high x 40" wide x 24" deep (from front of gas pipe). The flashlights, baseball and tennis equipment, punching bag, refrigerator and straw hats also shown were all part of the vast product line sold in the typical Winchester Store. From Tom Webster collection. Photo by T. Webster.

Values: $4,500 - $5,000
(gas range only).

Toaster, Ice Cream Freezer, Coffee Pot

Electric Toaster, One Quart Ice Cream Freezer, Six-Cup Electric Coffee Pot. The toaster (one of 5-6 found) has base 7 1/4" long and is 7 1/8" high. Tub of ice cream freezer (the smallest of six sizes) is 7 3/8" high. Coffee Pot (one of 3-4 found in this size) measures 9 5/8" high; the first nine-cup model was recently found. From Tom Webster collection. Photo by D. Kowalski.

Values: Toaster - $900 - $1,100; Ice Cream Freezer (One Quart) - $900 - $1,400; Coffee Pot (Six-Cup) - $2,100 - $2,500.

Red W Brand Paint Paddle Board

Paint Paddle Board. Hooks originally held "paddles" with paint colors on them. Fairly rare piece; very few paint-related displays have been found. Size is 18 1/4" wide x 6" high. From Curt Bowman collection. Photo by C. Bowman.

Values: $1,500 - $2,000.

Wood Cutlery Display

Wood Cutlery Display. Size is 17 7/8" wide x 12" high. From Dennis Mack collection. Photo by D. Mack.

Values: $500 - $900 (display only).

Parlor Stove

Parlor Stove. Steel exterior with baked-on finish hides the heavy cast-iron firebox. "We just about killed ourselves getting this upstairs," Tom Webster reports. Size is 44" high x 25" wide x 17" deep. Only two have ever been found. From Tom Webster collection. Photo by T. Webster.

Values: $2,750 - $3,000.

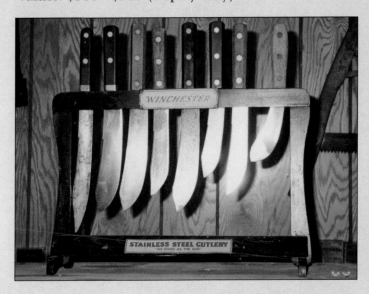

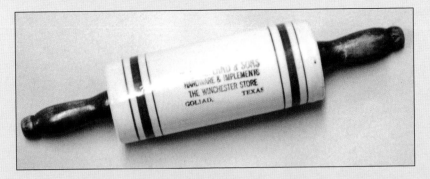

Rolling Pin

Rolling Pin. The only one ever found to date with a store name. Produced by W.E. Neyland & Sons in Goliad, Texas. Length from handle tip to handle tip is 15"; roll is 7 7/8" long. From Tom Webster collection. Photo by T. Webster.

Values: $2,200 - $2,500.

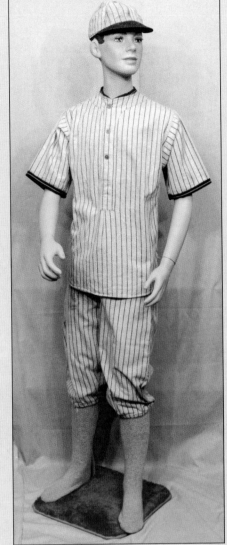

Crock Chicken Waterers

Crock Chicken Waterers - One Gallon and One Quart. One gallon waterer has base diameter of 10 1/8"; top diameter is 7 7/8"; height is 10". Base of one quart size has 6 7/8" diameter; top has diameter of 4 1/2"; height is 7". Back of this one gallon model shows Red Wing Pottery made it, so Red Wing collectors also want it. From Tom Webster collection. Photos by D. Kowalski.

Values: Quart - $2,800 - $3,000; Gallon - $2,000 - $2,200.

Baseball Uniform (Boy's)

Boy's Baseball Uniform. This is the only boy's cap ever found. From Tom Webster collection. Photo by D. Kowalski.

Values: $1,500 - $1,900 (Shirt, Pants and Cap).

Tennis Equipment

Tennis Racket, Case, Ball and Ball Can. All rare pieces. The tennis ball can is the only one ever found. It was finally opened in early 2000 to reveal three balls. The racket is unique because most of them had model names on them, such as "Precision" or "Leader" or "Ranger." This one simply has the "Winchester" logo on it. The case is unusual since most of them found to date have been a plaid pattern. This one also has two white buttons that read "Sportsmens Headquarters" around outside edge and "Winchester" across the middle. From Richard Hecht collection. Photo by R. Hecht.

Values: Can (full) - $7,500 - $8,500; (empty) - $3,000 - $3,500. Ball - $2,000 - $3,000. Racket - $1,500 - $2,500 (other rackets - $300 - $500). Racket Case - $600 - $800.

Fishing Plugs - Three Models in Eight Colors

Winchester produced three basic fishing plugs ... the Multi-Wobbler, the three-hook and the five-hook. Each style came in eight basic colors. The result was that a full set totaled 24 plugs. We present (right) a complete collection, created over several years, with every piece in excellent to mint condition. Colors (top to bottom) were: white with green back stripes, red head; green and gold back, yellow underneath; green with silver sides; scale finish - gold; red; crackle-back pattern; rainbow color; scale finish-silver. Photo compliments of Jim Muma.

Values: Multi-Wobbler - $500 - $700 (add 15 percent for the scale finishes, crackle-back and red heads); Three-Hook - $700 - $900 (add 15 percent for the scale finishes, crackle-back and red heads); Five-Hook - $850 - $1,200 (add 15 percent for the scale finishes, crackle-back and red heads).

Titan Casting Line

Titan Casting Line. Came rolled on two 50-yard spools in a box. Here's a pair of rolls with an extremely rare graphic of a jumping bass that is completely out of the water. One of the few pieces ever found with this bass on it. Photo compliments of Jim Muma.

Values: $400 - $500 (one spool with this rare graphic).

Scale Finish Gold - 3 Hook Fishing Plug

Scale Finish Gold - 3 Hook Fishing Plug (No. 9013). The scale finish and crackle back lures in the three different plug series were created by glueing a decal over the wooden body. This made them more subject to damage by water and more difficult to find in excellent condition. Here we see the scale detail. Photo compliments of Jim Muma.

From Cartridge Boards to Medals

Salesman Sample Kit - Metallic Cartridges

Salesman Sample Kit of Metallic Cartridges. The 52 cartridges include the .22 Extra Long, the .351 Self-loading (introduced in 1907), and the .401 Self-loading (introduced in 1910). Probably produced in the 1910-1920 era. Measurements closed are 16 1/4" long x 9" high x 1" deep. From Tim Melcher collection. Photo by TIM.

Values: $1,500 - $2,000.

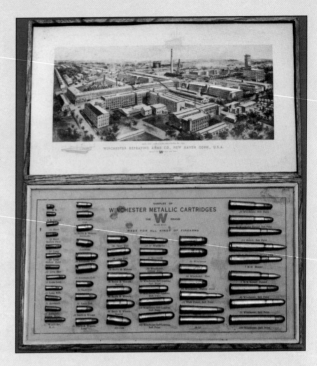

1874 Cartridge Board

Cartridge Board - 1874. The first Winchester cartridge board included only rimfire cartridges. Produced with wood frames. Less than five are known to exist. Overall size is 22" wide x 25" high; portion inside frame measures 19 1/2" x 16 3/4" deep. From Tom Webster collection. Photo by D. Kowalski.

Values: $10,000 - $12,000.

Wood Shell Case - Quail Cartridges

Wood Shell Case - Quail Cartridges. Loaded Star shotshell boxes with this label are very rare. This box label for 12 gauge shells is stamped "9 2 90" (September 1890). Case is 15 3/8" long x 10 1/4" high x 8 7/8" deep. From Tom Webster collection. Photo by D. Kowalski.

Values: $500 - $750.

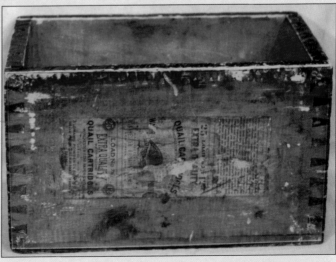

Salesman Sample Kit - Lubricants & Shells

Salesman Sample Kit. A rare combination of lubricants, cartridges and cutaway shotgun shells. Includes four very rare .410 gauge "window" shells. Probably produced in the 1906 - 1920 time period. Photos (below right) show close-ups of product. Measurements closed are 14" long x 7" high x 3" deep. From Tim Melcher collection. Photo by TIM.

Values: $1,500 - $2,000.

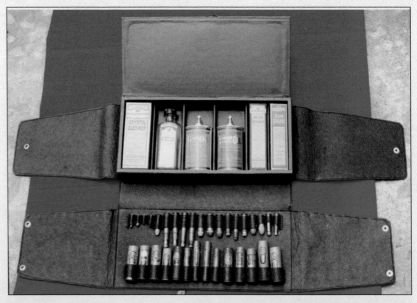

Glass Gun Cabinet

Glass Gun Cabinet. Probably produced during the 1920s. Only about five known to exist. Cabinet base is 17 3/4" square x 74 1/4" (from floor to peak). From Curt Bowman collection. Photo by C. Bowman.

Values: $4,000 - $5,500.

Model 58, Model 02 - Boxes

Boxes for Model 58 and Model 02. Early box for Model 58 which came out in late 1927. Model 02 box from same era (box style reportedly only made for a short time). The Model 02 was also one of the .22s offered as part of the Winchester Junior Rifle Corps kit. Each box measures 23" long x 4 3/4" wide x 1 7/8" deep. From Tom Webster collection. Photos by D. Kowalski.

Values: $500 - $750 (either box).

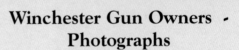

Winchester Gun Owners - Photographs

Woman with Dog, Young Black Man. Original photographs of Winchester gun owners. The elegant lady hunter (above) displays birds bagged with her Diamond Grade Model 97. Original photograph from 1909. Size is 7 1/8" wide x 9 1/2" high. Young black man (left) proudly holds his Model 90. Photo probably from same era. Size is 10 7/8" wide x 13 3/4" high. From Tom Webster collection. Photos by D. Kowalski.

Values: $100 - $150
(comparable original photographs).

Winchester Medals

Winchester Medals - display case. A portion of the Tom Webster collection. Some very rare pieces. For example, in the upper right corner is a gold watch fob (partially obscured by oval medal with "P" on it) that reads: "Presented to Burton Call. Salesman Leader CLVB 1924." It is one of only two known and would be valued at about $2,000.

Winchester Medals - close-up of lower left corner of display case. The medal in lower right with three head shots says: "Leaders at the Trap in 1912 Who Found the Win in Winchester - Allen Heil, W.R. Crosby, Fred Gilbert" - valued at $2,500 - $3,000. Next to it is the rarest of the Topperwein medals with the red "Winchester" in large letters under their picture - valued at $1,500 - $2,000. The medal with the figure skater (far left) may be the only one known; it says "World's Champion Ice Skater Bobbie McLean uses Winchester Skates" - valued at $700 - $800. Upper row shows various Winchester Junior Rifle Corps medals. Photos by D. Kowalski.

Shotgun Stock Tag

Shotgun Stock Tag. This one produced after 1906 (has large red "W"). At shooting competitions or the trap-shooting range, shooters used these to mark their guns. They might also have been awarded as prizes for high qualifying scores; the symbol reads "Medal of Award." The shotgun version is pictured. There is also another rarer rifle version. From Tom Webster collection. Photo by D. Kowalski.

Values: $100 - $150 (shotgun); $250 - $300 (rifle).

Magazine Advertising

Winchester magazine advertising has not yet become a serious aspect of Winchester collecting. But we predict it will. Magazine ads answer the needs of the collector with space problems and a limited budget. They're small, old, colorful and more plentiful than many other Winchester items. Prices are very reasonable. In fact, $20 or less should buy a broad selection of old ads.

Dating Winchester products and packaging can often be a real challenge. And different "experts" have made different guesses. However, these ads were chosen by Winchester as appropriate in timing and content for the magazine issue in question. We hope they help educate the collector community about some key dates.

All pictured ads are from the Tom Webster collection.

FOREST AND STREAM.   *Nov. 1907*   749

"LOOK FOR THE BIG RED W"

THE big red **W** is the connecting link between the consumer and the makers of Winchester goods. Over a year ago we adopted this safe-guarding trade-mark, and since that time every box, carton and package put out by us has borne the big red **W**, the hall-mark of goods as perfect as brains, experience and ingenuity, coupled with a modern and complete plant, can make them. Our object in adopting this trade-mark was to make it easy to distinguish Winchester goods from other makes, which equal them neither in quality nor reputation, and thus protect you and protect ourselves. We have done our part. Will you do yours by looking for the big red **W** whenever buying anything in our line? The big red **W** is to guns, cartridges and loaded shells what the word "Sterling" is to silverware the world over. For your own protection we again ask you to "Look for the big red **W**."

WINCHESTER REPEATING ARMS CO.,
New Haven, Conn., U. S. A.

Forest and Stream, November 1907

HOTCHKISS REPEATING RIFLE.

Simple, Effective and Durable.

Recommended by the Ordnance Board and adopted for service in the U. S. Army and Navy

6-Shot, and carries the Regular .45 Cal. 70 Grain U. S. Government Cartridge.

Price: Carbine, $22. Round Barrel Sporting, $25. Octagon Barrel, $27.

MANUFACTURED BY THE

WINCHESTER REPEATING ARMS COMPANY,

Send for Circular.   NEW HAVEN, CONN., or 312 BROADWAY, NEW YORK.

SOLE AGENTS FOR
COL. ANSON MILLS'
Woven Cartridge Belt.

The best belt in the market. Belts can be furnished for all sizes cartridges and for various gauges shot shells.

PRICE, $1.50. POSTAGE, 14c. ADDITIONAL.

Forest and Stream

Aug 1882

Forest and Stream, August 1882

The Companion, August 25, 1917

THE "LEADER"—The finest smokeless powder shell that science can produce. Made with a high brass base and unrivalled not only in quality of load but in variety of loads.

THE "REPEATER"—The standard smokeless powder shell, that gives superior service at medium cost. True to its great Winchester name in its power to cover, penetrate and stop.

THE "RANGER"—Winchester's solution of the shooter's problem of lowering the cost of the sport. Built of the best but held down in cost by standardization and limited loads. 12-gauge only with 23 loads, including a trap load.

The RANGER
A NEW *WINCHESTER* SHELL
TRADE MARK

USING SMOKELESS POWDER AND SOLD AT A POPULAR PRICE!

AT last! And Winchester has it first! A really high-grade smokeless powder shell at a low price!

Loaded with genuine DuPont No. 2 smokeless powder. Built on the same sound principles of balance and loading which have placed our Leader and Repeater Shells foremost in the confi-dence of hunters and trap-shooters.

The Ranger is sure fire—speeds fast —hits hard—makes a perfect pattern. Winchester offers it to sportsmen, to complete "the greatest shot shell trio in the world."

Always insist on Winchester Shells at your hardware or sport goods store.

WINCHESTER REPEATING ARMS CO., NEW HAVEN, CONN., U.S.A.

National Sportsman   *July 1924*

National Sportsman, July 1924

CLEAN as a WHISTLE

WHEN tired by a day of shooting —what a chore it used to be to clean a small bore rifle. Now—with Winchester Staynless Ammunition — you do not *have* to clean. Just take it easy when the day is done. Winchester Staynless Rim Fire Cartridges, you see, can neither rust, pit nor foul your barrel. Yet they retain all the old-time Winchester accuracy and dependability and, with any of the famous Winchester small bore sporting rifles, they form the ideal combination for .22 caliber shooting. In target work, of course, where Winchester

Model 52 is king, use the celebrated Winchester .22 Long Rifle Precision 75 (for indoors and the shorter outdoor ranges) and 200 (for the longer outdoor range). Or use Winchester Lestayn Rim Fire Cartridges combining Lesmok powder (for accuracy) with our Staynless priming to reduce rusting and pitting to the minimum. Winchester has also developed Staynless non-corrosive priming for Center Fire Cartridges. You can thus obtain maximum results in every kind of shooting with maximum protection for all rifles.

FREE—Winchester Guns and Ammunition are *made* for each other. To find the combination that gives best results in different kinds of shooting, write for your free copy of "The Game—The Gun—The Ammunition"—a most interesting guide for sportsmen.

WINCHESTER REPEATING ARMS CO., New Haven, Conn., U. S. A.

WINCHESTER
TRADE MARK

NEW—Model 58—a simple, dependable, single-shot, .22 caliber rifle — latest of Winchester small bore rifles and "every inch a Winchester" though it sells for only $5.50. (Anywhere in U. S.)

(Magazine Unknown), January 1928

CONVENIENCE
DEPENDABILITY

Note the added convenience of the new Leader box

WINCHESTER Lacquered Leaders, in their new handy-size flat boxes of ten shells, are now known not only as "the world's finest shotshell" but as the most *convenient* shotshell package.

The 10-shell carton—an innovation in shotshell packing introduced by Winchester—can be dropped in any side pocket without over-balancing the garment. Two or more of these cartons, in fact, slip into a space that will not comfortably hold *one* of the bulky 25-shell packages. And you can carry a variety of loads (each in its own box) with no loose shells to mix up or suffer damage in your pocket.

The 10-shell box is easier to open too. The flap-type cover can be flipped up with the thumb. With no seals to break, no separate cover to pull off, it's a one-handed job that saves time and temper when you're in a hurry for more ammunition.

Leaders (in their new box) and Winchester Speed-Loads, Repeaters and Rangers—are *all* shells which are noted for supreme dependability. Steve Crothers, famous trapshot, broke 1405 x 1410 (a phenomenal world's record) shooting Winchester Repeaters. In piling up this remarkable record he made one score of 499 x 500. You will find fast ignition, high velocity, consistent uniformity of pattern and certainty of fire at all temperatures in *every* grade and type of shell produced by Winchester.

As for guns, don't forget Model 21—the new double barrel shotgun which Winchester announced last month. It is a shotgun every lover of fine firearms will want to know and own. Standard grade, .12 guage—$59.50. Ask your dealer to show it to you and write for FREE booklets describing Winchester Guns, Ammunition, Flashlights, Roller Skates, Cutlery, Tools, and Fishing Tackle.

WINCHESTER REPEATING ARMS COMPANY
NEW HAVEN, CONN., U. S. A.

FITS the POCKET

EASY to OPEN

WINCHESTER

Model 21 — the outstanding new double gun — $59.50

Outdoor Life oct. 1930

(Outdoor Life), October 1930